How to
TELL FORTUNES
WITH CARDS

King of Clubs, King of Hearts, Queen of Diamonds, King of Spades.

BY WENZELL BROWN

BELL PUBLISHING COMPANY
NEW YORK

Contents

The publishers wish to thank the Atlantic Playing Card Co. of New York for use of its Cadette cards for the color photograph and other photographs of modern cards used in this book, and also the Victoria & Albert Museum for some of the Tarot card pictures.

0-517-126338

Manufactured in the United States Of America

Tarot cards pictured many gods, goddesses and symbols. Top left is a juggler with a wand (club), followed by a wheel of fortune (the circle of the wheel representing the heart suit). Next comes Juno, consort of Jupiter, with her wand and peacock. Lower left is Cupid ready to let loose his arrow into the hearts of the loving couple. The Emperor and Empress have their wands or sceptres as symbols of their office.

1. A Brief History of Playing Cards

The oldest "book" in the world was disguised as a pack of playing cards. This is *The Tarok of the Bohemians* and, spiritually, it is the ancestor of all packs of playing cards sold today.

Actually, although the origin of playing cards is lost in obscurity, it is certain that they pre-date the printed word. One popular legend claims that cards were invented in China in A.D. 1120 to entertain a concubine of the Emperor S'eun-Ho. Egyptian or Gypsy playing cards, developed separately, are probably many centuries older. They once formed an integral part of the worship of the Egyptian god, Toth. Their symbols, religious in nature, were used to foretell the future, to give advice and to pronounce the will of the gods. These cards were known as the *Tarot* (*Tarok* in German) or the Tablets of Fate. There can be little doubt that some version of these cards was consulted by the Israelites upon Divine Command as recorded in the *Book of Moses*.

Tarot cards were brought to Europe and made popular by the Gypsies, who used them for fortune telling, but it remained for the Crusaders to discover that cards could be adapted to games and gambling. The Crusaders introduced the cards to every capital of Europe and soon each country developed its own national version of the Tarot pack.

In most of the Tarot packs, each suit had 14 cards. Besides the King and Queen there were also the Knight and Page, which have been combined into the Jack of the modern pack. Some of the ancient packs had as many as 20 suits but, by the 13th century, they were fairly well standardized into four suits:

The Sun, The World, The Stars, The Moon, Judgment and Temperance on the old Tarot cards.

Swords which have become *Spades*.
Cups, Chalices or Circles which have become *Hearts*.
Dishes, Pentacles or Money which have become *Diamonds*.
Lances, Wands or Sticks which have become *Clubs*.

Originally there were 78 cards in the Tarot, including 22 unnumbered cards known as *atouts* or trumps. These were picture cards depicting scenes such as "The House of God," "The Wheel of Fate," "The Hanging Man," etc. In arcane law, these cards constituted the major oracles, while the numerical cards were the minor oracles.

The first known game of cards was called "The Game of Human Life." The cards were lined up on a board or table. Each player threw dice and moved a tab to the card designated by his throw. This game resembled closely the horse-racing games so popular at resort hotels and on ocean liners, except that the forfeits had a distinctly moralistic aspect. For example, the player whose dice stranded him on "The Drunken Man" lost two turns and had to return to "The Child at Two." The final card was called "Immortal Man" and the player who first reached this goal collected from his fellows.

Our puritan forefathers branded cards the instruments of the devil, but this is a relatively modern point of view. During the Renaissance many European countries outlawed all sports and games on Sundays with the specific exception of cards, which were considered edifying and "conducive to man's highest spiritual attainment." Perhaps the clue to the true value of cards can be found in the ancient *Book of the Tarok* which states that "good and evil when carried to the extreme fuse into one and become inseparable."

Even today the Gypsies claim that they possess "a secret book more ancient than any known to man, which is the one and only true guide to divination by the cards." If such a book exists, no copy has ever appeared outside the Gypsy world. It would seem more likely that the mysteries of Gypsy fortune telling have been handed down through the centuries by word of mouth.

From the dawn of their existence, cards have been credited with occult powers. It is interesting to note that, even in this day of scientific exploration into extra-sensory perception, the researchers at Duke University and other seats of learning have utilized cards as the best medium of experimentation.

Disputes, often acrimonious in nature, have raged over the centuries concerning the exact significance of the symbols employed in the Tarot cards. Cabalists, Knight Templars, Rosicrucians, Freemasons, Theosophists and countless scores of mystic and arcane cults have embraced these symbols and interpreted them in the light of their convictions.

As the author of this book, I have no intention of entering into learned and scholarly controversies, but I do want to point out that fortune telling by cards is not merely a game. Properly used, popular playing cards can provide an introduction to a philosophy and wisdom more ancient than any of the Western religions.

CHEVALIER DES BÂTONS

2. The Values of the Cards

Probably no two people who have ever read the cards interpret the symbols identically. The values which the Gypsies place on the cards are often diametrically opposed to the interpretations in ancient books of an esoteric nature. The Gypsies tend to over-simplify, to flatter and cajole. The esoteric cults, widely divided among themselves, give interpretations to the cards which are so complex and obscure as to be meaningless to the average individual.

In this book I have attempted to extract the basic meaning of each card and to present it in as simple and clear-cut a fashion as possible. Anyone who masters the material will be able to use the cards in forecasting his own future, or that of another, with a true understanding of the fundamentals underlying the symbolism of the cards.

To simplify matters, from this point on the person who reads the cards will be spoken of as the *Reader*. The person who consults the cards or seeks advice will be spoken of as the *Querent*. Use standard playing cards.

It should be stressed that fortune telling by cards is not based upon fatalism. It is rare indeed when the course of events cannot be changed. Most people have a series of problems with which they are wrestling. The sensitive Reader can bring these problems to the forefront. His task is not to dictate the actions of the Querent but to direct him into channels of thought which will clarify the nature of his problems and give him a deeper insight into his own personality and increased wisdom in dealing with the future.

3. Preparing for the Reading

Few Querents will come to the cards with any knowledge of the ancient religious symbols which they portray. In order to establish a rapport between the Reader and the Querent it is frequently desirable to discuss briefly the significance of these symbols. Actually, the cards in their original forms presented pictorial lectures in morality. The virtues which they sought to instill have common roots with all major religions. They urged kindness, courage, self-abnegation, tolerance, contemplation, completion, attainment, balance, an increased sense of beauty and symmetry, a recognition of law and order and, above all, a belief in the manifestation of a higher life force, the kinship of man's spirit with that of God.

The cards are symbols of this life force, but symbols only. The contemplation of these symbols is often beneficial to the troubled Querent. If the Querent approaches these symbols frivolously or with contempt, it may be well for the Reader to abandon the divination. Success in reading the cards depends largely on establishing a rapport in which the cards form a bridge linking the Querent and the Reader, so that temporarily they become part of a single entity. Thus the impact of the thoughts, the emotional responses and the reactions of the Querent are sensitized to a point where perfect communication becomes possible.

It is a common practice for the Querent to make a wish before the cards are spread out. The Reader may or may not conform to this custom but, if he does, he should be warned of its hazards. The wish is frequently frivolous and usually inadequately thought out, so that complications and ramifications occur which are likely to throw the reading off balance. The wish which is granted often proves disappointing and sometimes disastrous. Worst of all, the spread (of cards) which focuses about a specific wish, particularly a trifling one, must be interpreted in a somewhat superficial fashion.

Before touching the cards, the Reader should seek to divest himself of all malice, greed, pettiness, thoughts of vengeance or gain, and should be prepared to dedicate himself to the well-being of the Querent. Similarly, the Querent should be warned that if he seeks to use the cards for unworthy purposes, the oracles, while speaking truly, may misdirect and misguide him.

4. Laying Out the Spread

The Reader should handle the cards before offering them to the Querent to shuffle. He instructs the Querent to shuffle the cards slowly, thoughtfully and for some period of time. The proper way is not to break and riffle the cards, but to shuffle them with a rhythmic motion of the hands.

A tremendous number of spreads are used by diviners, most of which are highly complicated and many of which involve numerology, astrology or other occult sciences. I believe that if the rapport is firmly established, the formation of the spread is relatively unimportant. My personal preference is for the simple 15-card spread illustrated here.

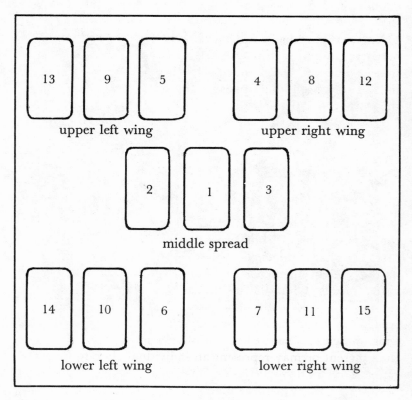

This may seem like an extremely simple spread, but 7,921,834,931,684,532,415,560,000 variations are mathematically possible! Thus the likelihood of duplication is so infinitely small as to be virtually inconceivable.

The Querent is told that he may hesitate in the shuffling

whenever he is so inclined, but the Reader makes the actual selection of the cards. He places the first card in the very middle of the spread, designated number 1 in the diagram.

The Querent continues shuffling the cards until he is ready for the second selection to be made. The Reader places this card in the position designated number 2 in the diagram. This continues until the entire 15 cards are laid out in the order shown.

No single card has a value all its own. It is influenced by the total spread and especially by those cards which are adjacent to it. Therefore the Reader should never comment on the individual cards as they appear, but should wait until he can get the *feel* of the entire spread.

5. The Positions in the Spread

By and large, the central card (number 1) represents either the Querent, his personality and the nature of his problems, or the primary influences which are moving through his life at the present moment. The cards which flank the central cards (numbers 2 and 3) are the next most important cards in the spread. They clarify the personality of the Querent and provide basic information regarding the situation in which he finds himself. A *face* card in the middle spread may represent the Querent or may represent an individual close to him who plays a dominating role in his life. The latter is more likely to be the case if the card ordinarily designates an individual of the opposite sex from the Querent.

The three cards in the upper right wing (numbers 4, 8, 12) indicate the course into which the Querent's life would normally flow unless checked by some positive action on his part.

The three cards in the upper left wing (numbers 13, 9, 5)

offer the Querent an alternate route which he may follow if he so desires. This wing designates possibilities which are open to him. Whether this alternate route is desirable or one which will be dangerous to him depends upon the cards themselves.

The three cards in the lower left wing (numbers 14, 10, 6) are generally guide posts which will assist the Querent in making his decisions. However, where the Querent is elderly, or past middle age, this wing is likely to represent elements in his past which affect his present or future circumstances. In the youthful Querent, these cards are more likely to forecast future events and offer advice as to how to prepare for them.

The three cards in the lower right wing (numbers 7, 11, 15) usually represent specific forces at work outside of the Querent. While these forces cannot be controlled, the Querent can adapt himself to them, thus utilizing them for his own advantage.

6. A Quick Run-Through of a Spread

Before proceeding further, let us look at a sample spread in order to examine its more salient features. Many more details about the individual cards involved will appear in later pages, but a quick run-through of a spread will give a rough idea of the usefulness of the cards.

This spread, which has been selected from copious files, is that of a young actress who came to consult the cards at a critical point in her career.

The advice which the cards offer in this case is extremely clear-cut. The central card (the Jack of Diamonds) obviously represents the Querent, for this card may be a young person of either sex who is on the threshold of life. To the right is the Three of Diamonds which often signifies a contract or business

Sample Spread.

opportunity. To the left is the Ace of Clubs, a card of dynamism and talent.

These three cards form the central core of the spread. In order to tell more of the character and personality of a Querent, the Reader must be familiar with the description of the Jack of Diamonds (page 69). To learn more of this particular Querent's talents, the Reader should consult the section dealing with the Ace of Clubs (page 83). These two cards will fuse together to give a picture of the Querent, and it is safe to assume that the contract or opportunity which lies open to her will be related to her skills and talents.

Next look at the upper right-hand wing of the spread. All the cards which appear there are beneficent and, grouped together in this fashion, promise wealth, fame, success, happiness and the achievement of lifetime ambitions. This wing represents the normal flow of the Querent's life. The advice here is for the Querent to continue on the path she is following and that, if she does so, she will have the opportunity to reap rich rewards.

Now examine the upper left-hand wing. This is an alternate route which she may take, but this route leads to failure! The warning is definite:

If the Querent fails to bend her energies in the direction which she has chosen and instead permits quarrels, petty misunderstandings and anger to influence her, they will divert her from the path of success. The Two of Spades represents a minor stumbling block which, badly handled, can have disastrous results. The Seven of Spades is a card of division, warning the Querent against discouragement and thoughtless actions. The Ten of Spades warns that neglect in concentrating on long-term objectives may result in unnecessary failures and disappointments. Obviously this alternate route must be avoided.

The next step is to examine the lower right wing of the spread. This wing represents outside influences which will affect the Querent's life. Here we see two Kings flanking the Ace of Diamonds. The Ace is a card of constructive power, symbolized by the magician, and often augurs success in the theatre or the arts. Usually Kings represent actual men, but the presence of two of them close together may indicate a group of people. The intimation here is that a number of individuals will be involved closely with the Querent and that they will give her assistance along the roadway which leads to success. Because these cards appear on the lower right wing of the spread and are joined to the central cards by a card of business (the Three of Diamonds), these men should not be interpreted in a romantic light, but rather as business associates.

The cards in the lower left wing of the spread warn that everything will not be smooth sailing. The two Fives suggest minor setbacks, tears, disappointments and periods of anxiety. However, the Nine of Hearts at the end of the spread promises that, if these obstacles are met with determination and courage, the Querent will achieve happiness beyond her highest expectations.

Having examined the individual cards and their position in the spread, the next step is to note whether any one suit dominates the spread. In this instance, the suits are distributed fairly equally. Therefore this phase of the reading is irrelevant.

The next check should be for three or more cards of the same numerical value. In this spread three Aces occur. As explained later in the book, three Aces, especially when accompanied by two Kings, promise unusual opportunities, much activity, changes, success, fame and the likelihood of mingling with many people in situations of unusual importance.

This is a first superficial reading of the spread. Many more subtle implications can be found by studying the sections of the book devoted to the individual cards and by concentrating on the juxtaposition of the cards in the spread.

Each spread offers a dual challenge to the Reader. He must

find not only its interpretation, but also ways to convey the information which the cards provide so that the Querent may derive the greatest benefit from the reading.

The Querent in this particular case has gone on to attain phenomenal success in her chosen vocation. She is well aware of the many instances where petty quarrels and discouragement could have blocked her career if she had not been forewarned of their danger.

Fortune telling is not merely a game. The ancient symbols represented by the cards were devised to assist mankind in attaining his noblest ambitions. For those who would use their skills in this area for the greatest advantage, the initial step is to master the meanings of each of the individual cards, the values of which are outlined in the following chapters.

The competent Reader must possess an intimate knowledge of each individual card in the pack so that it instantly flashes a message to him. It is important to know the significance of each card by heart, for the Reader who stops to look up a card or check it in the book risks losing the confidence of the Querent. He will find it hard to maintain the rapport essential to an adequate reading.

7. The Significance of the Individual Cards

In evaluating the cards, it should be stressed again that each card is shaded by those which surround it. The spread is an entity of which each of the 15 cards is an integral part.

Many of the cards have acquired some of the characteristics of the major cards (atouts) of the Tarot, which have been eliminated from the standard pack of playing cards. A particular challenge is offered by the Jacks because they serve the double purpose of the Knights and Pages of the Tarot.

As the Reader becomes more expert in divining the future through the cards, he will discover that certain cards take on special meanings or shadings in his hands. This is completely valid. According to Gypsy lore, "the oracle speaks to each diviner in a separate tongue."

Before turning to an examination of the individual cards, a final warning should be offered to the Reader. Many times the Querent will wish to discuss his problems at length with the Reader and may press him for direct advice. It cannot be repeated too often that the ultimate decisions must rest upon the Querent. The Reader should limit his responsibility to helping the Querent clarify his goals so that his actions will be motivated by considered judgment and in accordance with his own highest ideals.

8. The Joker

The Joker was originally "The Fool" of the Tarot cards. He represents a reversal of conventional standards, the independent spirit who walks alone, complete within himself, lacking all fear, guided by forces of nature and arcane wisdom.

In material affairs the Joker may stand for unconsidered actions, folly and eccentricity but, in spiritual matters, he represents originality, audacity and venturesome quest. It is said by the Gypsies that he "possesses the foolishness of God which is greater than the wisdom of men."

When the Joker appears in the middle of the spread, the indication is that the Querent has attained in some degree, or seeks to attain, freedom from physical restraints, grandeur of vision and the superior wisdom which men term folly. He is no longer bound by conventions and he has rid himself of pettiness, jealousy and covetousness so that he rises above human tragedy, pain or adversity to find a perfect unity of mind and spirit.

Obviously only on the rarest of occasions can such perfection be achieved. The presence of the Joker does not represent an accomplished fact, but brings to the Querent's recognition the tremendous spiritual forces with which he is surrounded. It highlights his aspirations to adapt himself to a mode of life in keeping with his noblest instincts.

Inevitably he will find himself bound by earthly restrictions, the nature of which may be indicated by the cards which adjoin the Joker.

When the Joker appears in the upper left wing of the spread, the indication is that the Querent will be faced with a choice of rejecting worldly goods to attain spiritual freedom, or of accepting material restrictions in order to assume social responsibilities.

On the lower wings of the spread, the Joker is likely to relate to more specific situations wherein the Querent may act in accordance with his highest ideals or may compromise with his conscience for personal profit, social acceptance or other practical reasons.

The Joker is also a warning that all is not as it seems, that there are hidden meanings beneath the obvious messages which can be read in the cards. Where the Joker appears, the Reader must take especial care in interpreting the spread and beware of pitfalls wherein a literal reading of the cards may lead to a reversal of truth. The Joker is a card of duality that tends to shroud the future in mystery.

(Caution to the Reader: It may be advisable for the relatively inexperienced Reader to omit any Jokers from the spread as its appearance complicates the reading. Also, care should be taken not to introduce a Joker into a used pack of cards because its relatively untouched surface may tempt the Reader or the Querent to select it when otherwise it would be rejected.)

LE MAT.

9. The Ace of Spades

There is a common superstition that the Ace of Spades augurs death or tragedy.

This is not true.

The Ace of Spades represents tremendous force, power and strength.

Whether this force operates for the benefit of the person whose future is being forecast, or against him, depends in large part upon the individual.

Some guidance as to the nature of this force may be found in the position of the Ace in the spread and the cards which adjoin it. With the Ace of Spades, high achievement becomes possible. If the strength is contained in the Querent, he can hold it in leash and find an inward power to face all obstacles in his path. He should look forward to the future with courage and surging hope. Adventures of the mind and spirit are his for the asking.

The Ace of Spades does represent a danger, too. Uncontrolled, the force can explode and destroy the Querent and those close to him. Where this Ace occurs, the Reader should explore its nature and prepare the Querent for rigid self-discipline and keen-sightedness in making beneficial use of the force at the opportune moment.

If the Ace lies in the middle of the spread, the force will dominate the subject's life. He has been granted great curative powers and should do well in medicine, nursing or allied fields. He has the capacity for leadership and should succeed in law, politics and other areas which demand dynamic energy. He is, however, likely to be plagued by narrow-mindedness, inflexibility and adherence to dogma. He should be encouraged to assume tolerant points of view and to dedicate his talents to his fellow men. He must curb his temper and his personal ambitions or else the force within him may become corrosive and bring about the enmity of other strong-willed individuals.

If the Ace of Spades lies in the upper right portion of the spread, it represents an external force which he will encounter. He should be prepared to cope with this force and use it for his own ends. If he is able to do so, he will emerge from the experience as a person of greater stature who has attained an inner security by his increased knowledge of his own capacities.

If the Ace lies in the upper left portion of the spread, the Querent may elect to bring this force into his life or to evade it. In this case the Reader should explore the capacities of the Querent to deal with new situations. The Reader may find that the Querent is on the brink of a decision. If he is timid, fearful and vacillating, he should be discouraged from making radical changes in his life patterns. On the other hand, if he is bold, self-assured and adventurous, unusual opportunities lie ahead for him. The decision must rest with the Querent, and he should weigh the risks of the course which he charts and decide for himself if he is ready to launch out on an interesting and challenging path, but one which is likely to be filled with hardships.

If the Ace of Spades lies on the lower wings of the spread, it is much more likely to relate to a specific instance where force may be employed. The adjacent cards will provide some clue as to the nature of the force. In this case the Querent should brace himself to weather an emotional storm; to meet an unexpected, explosive situation; or to withstand pressures from an overbearing individual. Success in dealing with a difficult situation may turn out to his advantage.

The life-giving force of the Ace of Spades is not evil. He who copes with it will find unexpected spiritual richness in his future.

10. The King of Spades

The appearance of the King of Spades in the spread indicates the presence of a man of powerful and dominating personality. He is likely to be highly intelligent, stable, ambitious, honest and motivated by practicality and reason.

If the Querent is male and the King appears in the middle of the spread, this may be an indication of his own personality. If the King appears in the wings, he is more likely to be a father, employer, staunch friend or advisor of the Querent.

When the Querent is a woman, the King of Spades represents a dominant male in her life. He may be father, brother, husband, friend or a man who seeks her hand in marriage. When the King lies in the middle of the spread, this man has had long association with the Querent. If the card lies in the right wing, the man has already entered into the Querent's life, though not necessarily in an important rôle. If the King lies in the left wing, this man will become known to the Querent at some future date.

Traditionally, the King of Spades has been represented as an older man of dark complexion. However, such a description is superficial. Black, in this case, does not refer to the man's coloration but to his positive nature, his virility and his capacity to control situations. Similarly, he need not necessarily be old but his outlook will be mature and not susceptible to change.

The King of Spades is likely to lack subtlety and to see things in terms of black and white. While he is well-intentioned, he may trample upon the sensitivities of others. He tends to be a good provider, astute in business affairs, well-liked and respected by his male associates. By his own code, he is generous, reasonable and kind. On the adverse side, he may be too sure of his own judgments, heavy-handed and either unwilling or unable to understand points of view which conflict with his own. He distrusts intuitive knowledge and tends to dismiss with contempt the artistic abilities, the soaring ambitions, the cherished dreams and idealism of those about him. Such attitudes may bring about domestic crises, create ill will in business, or antagonize friends.

If the Querent is represented by the King of Spades, he should be advised to give greater thought and consideration to those close to him. Inasmuch as he is a man of deep loyalties, kindly instincts and basic good will, he will desire to be fair and just. His preoccupation with material matters and getting things done will sometimes obscure his sense of the intricate pattern of other people's lives. If he can embrace a fresh view of spiritual and moral values, much added richness can enter his life.

If the spread indicates that the King of Spades is a man with whom the Querent must deal, he should be reminded of the many good qualities of the man, his staunchness, his loyalty, his uncompromising honesty. Above all, this man is governed by intelligence. Open opposition or carping criticism will only strengthen his determination to have his own way, but he will be susceptible to honest appreciation of his capabilities and able to understand conflicting viewpoints if they are represented in a reasonable, clear-cut fashion. He is deeply emotional, even sentimental, and when an appeal is made to his better instincts, he is highly responsive.

Such a man tends to think in concrete terms and usually does well in business, law or engineering. In spite of his outward appearance of competence, strength and domination, he has a great need for warm personal relationships and for a woman who will give purpose to his life. He does not like to be alone and, while he scorns open sentimentality, he cherishes any love or affection given to him.

25

The female Querent who ponders marriage or a business relationship with such a man should be advised to examine her own personality and attitudes with great care. This is not a man whom she can change or wrap around her finger. If she enters blindly into such a relationship, she may find herself broken by the experience. On the other hand, if she can promote the interests of this man and give him the warmth and emotional security which he needs, she can expect his lifelong devotion to her comfort and happiness.

11. The Queen of Spades

Superficially, the Queen of Spades represents a dark woman.

But the darkness does not refer to coloration, nor does it indicate evil as is sometimes supposed.

The Queen of Spades is a woman of unsuspected depths, whose immediate personality may be misleading. Such a woman, especially as she grows older, tends to conceal her emotions beneath a cloak of calmness which may make her appear unemotional and haughty or even shallow and unresponsive. This woman is not easy to know, but the cultivation of her friendship will be rewarding. Once this friendship is won she will offer unswerving loyalty and unselfish devotion. On the other hand, she may become an implacable enemy, ruthless and cruel.

Such a woman should be approached with complete sincerity, for she is highly intuitive and will be quick to recognize deceit or ulterior motives. Unless the Querent can meet her with frankness and a genuine desire to secure her friendship, it is best to avoid her.

While the Queen of Spades is a woman of deep emotional

responses, her appearance in the layout rarely indicates romance. She is much more likely to play the role of mentor, advisor or confidante. However, where there is romantic attachment between her and the Querent, she will be a woman of endless surprises—passionate, possessive, inclined to jealousy.

Because she is psychic, she often possesses knowledge gleaned through telepathic sources and her advice should be listened to with care. Her critical faculties are acute, and her intuitive knowledge of persons is likely to be sound unless prejudiced by personal affront. Many successful people have a Queen of Spades in their lives and this is particularly true in the field of arts. She provides a practical, stabilizing influence upon whom the gifted may depend. She is frequently the source of inspiration, the spur to fame or success, the demanding critic who will not permit failure. She has the tendency to dominate and to appear aggressive and unfeeling but she can easily be won over by affection, good nature and respectful consideration of her views. Once such an emotional bond is established, she is unstinting in her generosity and self-sacrifice.

Conversely, if she is antagonized, she is a dangerous enemy. Her intuitive powers are sharpened to find every weakness and flaw in her adversary. Guided by some psychic force, she finds ways to hurt, humiliate or injure the individual who has offended her.

The complexity of her nature will make her appear mysterious and enigmatic, driven by vagaries, subject to insights hidden from others and capable of contradictory actions.

But she is a woman well worth cultivating.

She must be accepted graciously—or scrupulously avoided.

12. The Jack of Spades

The Jack represents a young person, but the sex is not indicated by the card itself. In the original Tarot cards, each suit had 14 cards, including a "Knight" and a "Page." At a later date, the Knight and the Page were combined into the Jack. In early divination, the Knight represented a youth of the opposite sex from the Querent, while a Page represented a young person of the same sex.

Because the Jack has a double identity, the Reader must depend to some extent on intuition in determining whether this card represents a suitor, a friend, a relative or the Querent's object of love.

If a Jack faces a Heart or Club, it usually means that the person is of the opposite sex of the Querent. If it faces a Spade or a Diamond, the indication is that the Jack represents someone of the Querent's own sex. If the Jack is the end card on the middle line of the spread, the suit of the card above may determine its sex. If the Jack is at the extreme end of one of the wings and looks outward, the indication is that the individual represented will be going out of the Querent's life. Whether this departure is fortunate or not, will depend on the card closest to the Jack.

(NOTE: This explanation concerning the way the Jack faces is the same in all suits, so it will not be repeated in each case.)

The Jack of Spades represents a young and frequently immature person. The delineation of character cannot be as complete as in cards representing older persons. By and large, if it is determined that the Jack represents a male, he will develop characteristics somewhat similar to those of the King of Spades. Similarly, if the individual is female, she is likely to possess many of the personality traits of the Queen of Spades.

However, these characteristics are usually modified. The Jack of Spades is always a friendly person. If he is a young man, he tends to be dynamic, alert and often brilliant. He is restless and filled with nervous energy which may take the form of athletic prowess or intellectual curiosity. However, his interests tend to be short-lived and much of his energy may be wasted. His capacities are undeveloped and he needs ballast to settle down to life. The female Querent interested in such a youth should examine herself to see if she can offer this stabilizing influence. If she herself is unstable, insecure or given to quick temper, the alliance may be marked by quarrels, unhappiness and eventual separation. On the other hand, if she is able to leash his energies and direct them into constructive channels, so that a true alliance is formed between them, contentment and success may evolve from the union.

If the Querent has doubts, she should be advised to delay her decision. She should also be encouraged to discuss long-term plans with this young man. While he may appear to her in romantic guise, he is essentially practical and wants a helpmate who will implement his progress towards the goals which he has set for himself.

Where the Querent is a young man and the Jack of Spades appears in the spread in such a way as to designate a young woman, he will find that he is due for a series of surprises. Outwardly this girl may appear placid, but she will possess unexpected depths of character which will be revealed gradually. She is ardent, intuitive and inclined to be fiercely possessive. She will have many facets to her personality, some of which will appear contradictory. On the surface she may be wilful, capricious and given to flights of fancy. But her shifting moods cloak a determined character in which direct goals have been established. She is ambitious, skilled in directing others and her loyalty, once given, will never alter. She may achieve her ends by flattery, cajolery and subterfuge but, at the same time, she will be warm, generous and capable of tremendous sacrifices for those whom she loves.

Such a woman cannot be taken by storm. She must be wooed with diligence over a prolonged period. A young man may be fortunate to find such a partner with whom to share his life, but he should be warned that not all the surprises in store for him will be pleasant ones.

13. The Ten of Spades

The Ten of Spades symbolizes a wall or barrier. In spiritual matters it may mean the end of a delusion, the recognition of false goals, the surrender to the inevitable or the abandonment of long-cherished plans. The acceptance that a certain phase of life is finished may be difficult. The individual may feel disappointed, bitter or humiliated. The person who hurls himself recklessly against the wall, who blames others or who wallows in self-pity, may shatter his life. On the other hand, a calm appraisal of the situation may lead to a new and better set of values, to increased spiritual strength and to fresh pleasures from which frustrating and unrewarding ambitions have been removed.

When the Ten of Spades is the outer card in one of the wings of the spread, the indication is that some course of action which has appeared open will either close or lead to a dead end. Where this formation occurs, the Querent should be urged to review his plans for the future with the possible idea of revising them. The Reader should take the utmost care against advising the Querent to abandon any given set of plans. He should, instead, encourage the Querent to explore alternate routes and not to commit himself so fully to a single hope or ambition that he becomes blind to all other objectives. The pathway that is blocked may lead to unhappiness or even tragedy; therefore, the barrier may be a blessing in disguise.

When the Ten of Spades lies in the middle of the spread, it is an indication of important news which will alter the course of the Querent's life. It is also likely that some person as yet unknown to the Querent will play a significant role in his future. The Reader's judgment in assessing whether this new influence is benign or otherwise must be based in part upon the surrounding cards, but the Querent is the final, decisive factor. His reaction to a frustrating and disappointing situation is the keynote to his enduring happiness. He need not know lasting defeat because one passage is barred, but it may require wisdom and courage to seek a new pathway to happiness.

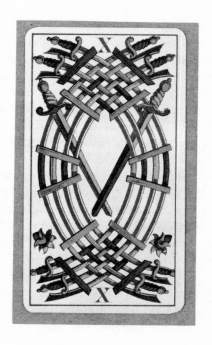

14. The Nine of Spades

Traditionally the Nine of Spades spells catastrophe. It is linked with the collapse of the Tower of Babel, the stroke of lightning, the swift destructive forces of evil, the overthrow of long-established patterns of living and the necessity to abandon well-laid plans.

This, however, is only partly true.

The Nine of Spades indicates changes through unexpected and unpredictable sources. But it may also destroy outworn patterns and free the Querent from the chains of customs which have bound him for so long that he has grown unaware of their weight and the restrictions which they impose upon him.

The danger lies, not in the destruction of that which is old, but in the failure to prepare for that which is new. The Nine of Spades, when found in the middle of the spread, is a clear-cut warning that the Querent should broaden his horizons, seek out new friends, accept new ideas. He should move forward into life instead of retreating, for the past cannot be recaptured. The severance of old bonds may be painful, but the future lies ahead, uncharted, with myriad routes which the Querent may explore.

The Nine of Spades is a card of fear, but fear that may be overcome. In the youthful Querent it may mark the first tenuous steps in leaving the shelter of family life. In the older Querent it may indicate the breaking up of the home, the loss of security and a radical revision of his life plan. Where this card appears in a prominent position in the spread, the Querent should be advised to seek out new interests. It may be wise for him to turn his back deliberately on the past and to make radical departures from his routine of life. He should voluntarily cast off old prejudices and habits of thought which impede his progress. To continue without change may be calamitous.

On the other hand, if the Nine of Spades appears in either of the left-hand wings, he has a choice of maintaining his present course of life or of altering it. The cards which accompany the Nine in the wing should guide the Reader in assessing the desirability of change.

15. The Eight of Spades

The Eight of Spades is a card of contentment. It represents a haven or refuge from worldly cares, a surcease from competition and trouble. It is a card of quiet pleasure, rest and relaxation. This calm joy may be found through the relationship with another person or it may be related to a place or some kind of activity such as a hobby or sport. The cards which surround the Eight should give the Reader some clues as to the nature of this benign force.

However, the Eight of Spades represents only a facet of the Querent's life. It is not a total card. The comfort, the pleasure which lies within the Querent's grasp is a part-time thing, a segment of his life which is separated from the mainstream of his daily activities.

The Querent should be warned against too great a dependency on this quiet pleasure. If he seeks to withdraw into a state of torpor and complete relaxation, thereby neglecting responsibilities, he may be due for a rude awakening in which he finds his world shattered.

The pleasure is there for the taking but to keep his refuge safe, he should wall it off from the rest of his life and remain vigilant lest he become imprisoned by his own sybaritic tendencies.

16. The Seven of Spades

The Seven of Spades is a card of division. It indicates partial success in the plans or aspirations of the Querent. It is also a warning of unexpected turns and twists of fate. Where the Seven of Spades appears, the Querent may find that objectives which he has successfully achieved do not bring expected satisfactions and rewards! The Querent should be advised to re-evaluate his plans and to view them with greater objectivity. The pathway ahead is, in all likelihood, strewn with more difficulties than he realizes. He must expect setbacks but, if he can weather these disappointments, he can achieve some of his goals. He should be cautioned not to give up too easily. Above all he should not act in pique in such a way that he destroys future opportunities. The Reader should remind him, in as tactful a way as possible, that success which comes too easily loses its meaningfulness, while success which comes after many hardships and sacrifices gives enduring pleasure.

17. The Six of Spades

The Six of Spades is a card of anxiety. It usually marks a period of suspended motion in which the Querent can do little but wait. This may be a period of sickness either for the Querent or someone close to him. More often, however, it is a time during which the Querent awaits decisions made by others which he feels will be handed down to him. Because of this he is liable to feel trapped by circumstances and to cease his activities until he receives further information.

The Reader must be guided by the cards surrounding the Six of Spades in judging whether or not the period of anxiety will end happily or unhappily for the Querent. However, the Reader should take note that the outcome desired by the Querent and that which is truly desirable are not necessarily the same.

The Querent should be advised that, during the period of anxiety, he should examine all facets of the problem and make certain that he has done everything possible to bring about the desired ends. Once he has done this he should attempt to dismiss the problem by plunging into other interests so that, when the decision is rendered, he is best capable of accepting it if it is adverse or benefiting by it if it is propitious.

18. The Five of Spades

The Five of Spades is the card of separation. Its appearance in the middle of the spread is likely to mean that the Querent will break old ties, change employment, settle in a new location or travel extensively. Inherent in the Five of Spades is a sense of grief, sorrow and sometimes remorse. Traditionally the Five of Spades is associated with tears but, in most cases, the change is voluntarily made. The sorrow which comes from leaving old friends may be compensated by meeting new situations, finding enlarged patterns of experience and constructing a more pleasurable life.

The separation may be symbolic or spiritual rather than physical. Ideas previously accepted may be rejected. Concepts may change. Prejudices may evaporate. Long established judgments may alter. Illusions may die.

The cards close to the Five of Spades indicate the nature of the separation and whether it will bring eventual joy or sadness to the Querent. If the separation is born of quarrels, bitterness or strife, the Reader should advise the Querent to examine his plans for change and not to act with precipitation or through anger. If he can divorce himself from undesirable reactions to what may seem an intolerable situation, it is possible that the separation can take place with a minimum of grief and ill will.

When the Five of Spades appears in the upper right wing of the spread, it frequently means that someone close to the Querent will depart from his life or that a situation with which he has long been familiar will change. If the Five of Spades is flanked by Diamonds, the indication is a shift of business relationships. If the Five of Spades appears in the upper left wing, the separation will be optional. The two remaining cards of the wing will hint at the effects of the change should the Querent decide to follow this pattern.

If the Five of Spades appears in the lower wings of the spread, the indication is that the separation will be incidental to other matters. The person or situation removed from the Querent's life may be of importance only in that it affects his business, finances or social life.

Under no circumstances is the Five of Spades a card of death. At its worst this card may mean loss of friendships through quarrels, vituperation or anger. Frequently a swift clean-cut cleavage from an established pattern of life is preferable to maintaining a situation fraught with petty annoyances, irritation, bickering, distrust and other forms of unpleasantness.

Because radical change and separation from friends, family or employment always involve unforseeable dangers as well as opportunities, it is unwise for the Reader to make positive recommendations. His advice should be restricted to guiding the Querent toward the recognition of his innermost feelings so that he will not take irrevocable steps before testing their advisability against his mature judgment.

19. The Four of Spades

The Four of Spades is a card of recuperation or healing. It may mark the end of a period of sickness, prolonged anxiety or strife.

On the surface this may appear to be a period of wasted time and energy, but in actuality it is a pause to renew strength. On the physical plane, the Four of Spades indicates a time of convalescence after which the individual will be restored to health. On the spiritual level it indicates a cessation of uncertainty, indecision and futility. Quiet and rest will result in fresh beginnings, renewed determination, deeper insight and richer concepts of living.

20. The Three of Spades

The Three of Spades is a card of sudden resolution, the swift decision to take action in a seemingly minor matter. Whether this decision will be made by the Querent or by some other person in such a way as to affect him depends upon the position of the card in the spread. In either case the decision may be, or appear to be, motivated by vindictiveness or spite, rather than sustained judgment.

If the Three of Spades appears in the middle of the spread, the Querent should be advised not to let personal animosity warp his critical faculties. In reacting too strongly to petty annoyances he may destroy the success of long-term objectives.

Where the Three of Spades occurs in juxtaposition to a face card he may be the victim of a slur or an unfair appraisal of his intentions by another person. While this may cause him grief and stir up his resentment, he should be prepared to react with generosity and not to counter the injustice with angry denials, an exchange of accusations, threats or tears. He should be advised to lay the matter to one side until he can regard it objectively and determine whether the difficulty can be adjusted or if it should be ignored.

The Three of Spades may actually forewarn the Querent of a test or trial of his capacity to deal with unpleasant matters. Success in so doing may lead to improved conditions in business, better personal relationships and increased respect among his associates. Therefore, although the Three of Spades may forewarn of an episode which is temporarily disagreeable, it may be one which will work out to his benefit.

Whenever the Three of Spades occurs in the spread, it is wise to explore the situation more deeply. As the Querent may have no knowledge of the shape that this minor misfortune may assume, he can be caught off balance and act to his own detriment. The Reader should discuss the problem with him in abstract terms in order that he may achieve a state of mind that will be helpful at the moment when he must cope with an irritating, humiliating or disappointing situation.

21. The Two of Spades

The Two of Spades represents a minor stumbling block in one's path, sometimes no more than a trifling irritation or a brief delay. However, its appearance in the spread is a warning that should not be overlooked. The petty annoyance that is met cheerfully and patiently can be handled easily, but if impatience gives way to bad temper, obstinacy or vindictiveness, the original trifle may assume unreasonable proportions and even destroy carefully laid plans.

When the Two of Spades appears, and especially so if it is centrally located, the subject should be forewarned so that he will meet the block calmly and not come upon it unprepared. Courtesy, consideration of others and a quiet appraisal of the difficulty, may well mark the difference between eventual success or failure in a cherished project.

If the Two of Spades is centrally located it also indicates that the minor difficulty will appear in the near future. The Two often conceals an incident of unrecognized importance upon which the future may hinge although the subject remains unaware that this is so.

22. The Ace of Hearts

The Ace of Hearts is a card of pleasure. It promises joy, merriment, love and fertility. However, when badly placed in the spread, it can be a warning of dissipation, waste, and a sacrifice of spiritual values for transitory pleasure.

Like all Aces, it is a card of explosive force. It may predict strong, romantic attachment, birth or re-birth of spiritual faith and joy.

When found in the middle of the spread, the joy will be an integral part of the Querent's personality. If there are a number of face cards or tens in the spread, the Querent will have the opportunity for new, varied and pleasurable social contacts. He will be the hub of festivities and he will possess friends whose regard for him is much greater than he realizes.

If the Ace of Hearts is flanked by Clubs, the joy is likely to be more subdued, to be accompanied by peace and quiet joy. When there is a preponderance of Diamonds in the spread, there is a promise of business success and increased satisfaction in work.

When the Ace of Hearts lies in the lower left wing of the spread, the indication is that the Querent is an object of love, adulation or devotion of which he is not aware, or which he does not reciprocate. Especially where the central cards are Spades, the Querent may feel himself unloved because he has not taken time to cultivate the people around him or has failed to do so through shyness, cynicism, preoccupation with personal affairs or because he has underestimated his own capacity to win the love of others.

Whenever the Ace of Hearts appears it should be accepted as a challenge to share joy with others. It indicates that the Querent has not taken full advantage of the gifts with which he has been endowed.

Traditionally, the Ace of Hearts is the card of young lovers and gives promise of marriage and children. However, this is too literal a concept. Love has many facets. It is the unifying force that draws people together in happiness. It is interesting to note that in early Tarot cards, love was depicted in a three-fold pattern: joy in one's self, love of another and the outward spreading of the love to enfold many others. Only when love contains all three of these aspects is it complete.

Where the Ace of Hearts dominates the pack, the Querent should be advised to extend his circle of friends. He is gifted in bringing to the surface the latent good in others. He should do well in social work, the ministry, teaching or any other business or profession which brings him into contact with large numbers of people.

When the Ten of Spades stands between the Ace of Hearts and a face card, the indication is that a barrier exists which prevents a satisfying relationship with another person but that the barrier can be swept aside. The Reader should advise the Querent to give serious thought to this problem, for its satisfactory solution will add to his own happiness.

When the Nine of Spades lies beside the Ace of Hearts or blocks one of the wings, the Querent should be warned that a situation which imperils his happiness exists. Perhaps his joy has blinded him so that he has given unwitting offense to others or failed to take safeguards to protect himself from misfortune. If this is so, he would be wise to make a sober appraisal of his situation to assure a more permanent happiness.

23. The King of Hearts

The King of Hearts represents a man of boundless good will and integrity. He is straightforward, dependable and mild-tempered. Outwardly he is uncomplicated and frequently conceals his feelings with gruffness; often he is inarticulate, his kindness being shown by deeds rather than words. Because of this, he may be regarded as insensitive and incapable of understanding the more intricate personalities of others.

When the Querent is a woman or a young man, the King of Hearts may appear as the father image or the symbol of authority. He is the solid rock to which their lives can be anchored. While the King of Hearts usually represents an older man, this is not so much a matter of age as maturity of judgment, tolerance and wisdom.

The male Querent who finds the King of Hearts in the middle of the spread may have such a disposition or he may aspire to develop the exterior calm and other characteristics which he admires in some older and more experienced man.

The female Querent, in the middle of whose spread the King of Hearts occurs, will find that her life is, or can be, intimately interwoven with such a man. He may be husband, father, devoted admirer or even, in some cases, a loving son.

When the King of Hearts appears in the upper left-hand wing, the indication is that such a man will enter the Querent's life in the not-too-distant future. The Querent will have the choice of accepting this man's aid and loyalty, which may be coupled by restraints and obligations, or of rejecting him.

When the King of Hearts appears in the upper right-hand wing, he will become a potent force in the Querent's life. But his friendship can only be won through the integrity of the Querent. The King of Hearts is a man who rarely shows animosity but he will be vigorous in his opposition to dishonesty, evasion of responsibility or other violations of his moral code. Should he be openly flaunted, he will strike back with courage, determination and sometimes with crushing force.

When the King of Hearts appears in the lower wings of the spread, he is more likely to be a man who will enter the Querent's life temporarily, but he may be instrumental in altering the entire life pattern. Often he is a man in a position of authority. He may pave the way for business promotion, sit in judgment of the Querent, or act as mentor or guide in domestic or social situations. He may provide financial assistance or emotional ballast in periods of stress.

The King of Hearts' outer calm may be misleading. He is often far more complicated than he appears. However, his lack of guile and his tendency to trust others may prevent his success in business or finance. He is admirably suited to teaching, judiciary posts, the ministry or any position which requires unswerving honesty, restraint and considered judgment.

Where the King of Hearts lies beside a Jack—especially if the Querent is a woman—the indication is that the woman is seeking to instill strength of character, courage and a sense of responsibility in some younger person. This being so, inevitably the woman possesses some of the admirable characteristics attributed to this card. It may also be suggested that she should find some older man, symbolized by the King of Hearts, to guide and assist her.

The King of Hearts is rarely of a creative turn of mind, but he will possess a love of beauty and will find joy in simple things.

In all other suits but Hearts, marriage between the King and Queen of the same suit is likely to be disastrous. But the King and Queen of Hearts are admirably mated. Each will give to the other absolute love and trust and, while neither may recognize the subtleties of the other's nature, their lives will be rich and full in reciprocated love.

24. The Queen of Hearts

The Queen of Hearts offers pleasure, joy, unstinting and unquestioning love. She is deeply emotional, and acts through instinct rather than reason. Traditionally she is jolly, light-hearted, frivolous and gay. But she is fruitful too. While she may lack intellectual depths, she sparks ideas and serves as an inspiration to more talented people about her. She is highly sensitive to the moods of those who are fortunate enough to win her love and, through her trust and belief in them, encourages them to fulfill their desires, ambitions and aspirations.

While she lacks creative skills, she is attracted to the arts and has a deep sensitivity for beauty in any form. Although her judgments may be at fault, she errs on the side of generosity. She is never petty or mean but she can be stubborn and wilful. She responds quickly to kindness but is inclined to be easily hurt. She lacks aggression and is often impractical where her own affairs are concerned, but will show tremendous moral and physical courage in defending the objects of her love.

On the surface, the Queen of Hearts appears practical and primarily interested in creature comforts. She is a good home-maker, an excellent cook and a devoted mother. Beneath the surface, however, she may lead a secret life filled with fantasy, aspirations and soaring ambitions for those she loves. There is an undercurrent of melancholy which she rarely shows. Her love is paralleled by enduring grief for the misfortunes which befall others and the imperfections of life.

She is a champion of the underdog, a friend to the friendless, a crusader for justice. But she is frequently mistaken and easily imposed upon. She tends to over-evaluate people, both in the matter of skill and character. She can see no flaw in those she loves. Her own lack of subtlety blinds her to duplicity in others. Her honesty impels her to move directly to a point and sometimes to be blunt and tactless. She is outspoken in anger, but easily appeased and never bears a grudge.

Usually she is sunny in disposition, given to laughter and small talk. She loves companionship and takes great joy in life's minutiae. Small gifts are of great importance to her and she is deeply moved by kindness. Her principal preoccupation lies in creating pleasures for others, especially the inner circle of her home and friends.

When the Queen of Hearts lies in the middle of the spread of a female Querent, the indication is that she possesses many of the characteristics symbolized by this card. Where the other cards in the spread represent hardship, deceit or danger, this is a warning that the Querent should proceed cautiously. She should be advised against too ready acceptance of others at their face values. If a Diamond appears at the right of the Queen, she must guard herself in financial matters. If the Ten of Hearts appears at her right, she will find deep joy in a younger person, possibly in the success of a son but more likely in her close relationship with a child.

If the Querent is a male and the Queen lies in the middle of the spread, it signifies that he is deeply loved. In this case the Queen may symbolize an entire family. If the Queen lies in the upper right or left wings of the spread, an opportunity for great happiness will soon be open to him. If the Queen lies in the lower wings of the spread, he will meet a woman who will offer him great comfort.

While the Queen is usually a mature woman, this may be a maturity of mind, not of years. The youthful Querent—regardless of sex—in whose spread the Queen appears, is promised the gift of a satisfying and rewarding love, though not necessarily in the immediate future.

25. The Jack of Hearts

The Jack of Hearts is the card of romance. Also it is the card of folly and thoughtless abandonment to pleasure.

Where the Jack of Hearts appears, the Querent may expect a carefree interlude between the more serious pressures of life. This may mean an affair of the heart, but not necessarily so. It can represent a happy holiday, pleasant friendships, a round of parties or some other amusing break from the monotony of routine work.

When the Jack of Hearts lies in the middle of the spread, it may serve as a warning to the Querent to take life more seriously, to look towards the future and to avoid hedonism. The Jack of Hearts is easily tempted to excesses in eating and drinking and tends towards self-indulgence. He is by nature generous and fond of people, so that he must take care lest he become involved in unpleasant situations through his impulse to please others.

If the Jack lies in the inner corner of any of the wings, the indication is that the Querent will meet a person whose gaiety will charm and disarm him. This association may be pleasant, stimulating and even valuable to the Querent, but he shoul not take the situation too seriously. If there is a romantic interlude, it should be entered into lightheartedly for the Jack of Hearts is likely to be inconstant and mercurial in temperament—here today and gone tomorrow. When the Jack faces a Spade, especially a Seven or Ten, there is a clear-cut warning of disappointment or heartbreak for the Querent if he dallies too long amid pleasures.

On the other hand, where the Jack of Hearts appears at the end of a wing, the Querent may look forward to a rewarding period of joy which will mark the success of some enterprise for which he has worked long and hard.

CHEVALIER DES COUPES   VALET DE COUPE

26. The Ten of Hearts

The Ten of Hearts is a messenger and the news which he brings is usually good. The message, however, is likely to be a turbulent one, upsetting routine and raising havoc with carefully laid plans.

The Ten of Hearts is a card of optimism which will send the spirits of the recipient soaring, but he should be warned that his happiness may be temporary. Though he rejoices, he should avoid any reckless action which may jeopardize his future.

A clue to the nature of the message should be found in the cards close to the Ten. A King or Queen on either side of the Ten may mark a reunion with old friends. In the same way, Jacks or Eights indicate meetings with young people, or new friendships. Diamonds indicate that the message will relate to money, while a preponderance of Hearts in the spread augurs marriage, issue, or in the case of older people, grandchildren.

If the Two or Ten of Spades precedes the Ten of Hearts in the spread, the indication is that good news will follow news which was initially bad. There will be a happy conclusion to a matter which had appeared to bring only sadness. Conversely, if the Ten of Spades follows the Ten of Hearts in the spread, the joyous news may prove to be false. If the Two of Spades is in this position, there may be a letdown or minor disappointment after the original elation which the good news has created.

27. The Nine of Hearts

The Nine of Hearts represents happiness beyond all expectations. If the Querent has made a wish, the Nine of Hearts does not promise fulfillment of this wish as expressed in the Querent's mind. Instead, it represents something greater and more enduring, extending far beyond the realm of the Querent's imagination.

In many ways the Nine of Hearts is the most joyous card in the pack. It represents spiritual well-being, an inner growth, contemplation, self-knowledge and an alliance with the life forces. Inherent in the Nine of Hearts is the warning that these values can be thrown away unless the Querent sincerely seeks wisdom beyond himself. The happiness may be destroyed by greed, avarice, spite, envy or too great a preoccupation with material matters.

When the Nine of Diamonds appears in the same spread as the Nine of Hearts, the indication is that long-cherished ambitions or life-long aspirations will reach fruition. There will be a perfected balance between inner calm, contemplation, increased self-regard and the more materialistic rewards of wealth, fame, public recognition and pleasurable excitement.

When the Nine of Hearts is adjacent to a face card, the indication is that this happiness may come through another person or be shared with him. If the Three of Diamonds separates the Nine of Hearts from a face card, there is a warning that the element of jealousy may be present. The Querent should be advised to use utmost tact in order that his happiness may not be marred by causing unnecessary grief to another.

When the Nine of Hearts lies in a spread in which Spades predominate, the Querent may find growth, increased stature, maturity and wisdom in the midst of difficulties or hardships. In this case, the Nine of Hearts is a symbol of victory over misfortunes, which will give the Querent strength, insight and recognition of himself as a person capable of facing adversity with courage and generosity.

The Nine of Hearts is symbolized by a key which opens many doors. It is the key to the awareness of one's self as a person, inviolable and separate, who can rise above circumstances and find joy and peace in the knowledge of his own integrity.

28. The Eight of Hearts

The Eight of Hearts represents a gift which causes pleasure. Whether the gift is received by the Querent or given by him to another depends upon the place of the card in the spread. The gift is not necessarily material. It may be the gift of love, restored health, spiritual knowledge, wisdom or ease of mind. Whatever it is, the gift should not be ignored, because only to the extent that it is treasured will it give happiness.

Where the Eight of Hearts lies in the middle of the spread, an exchange of gifts is indicated. Herein the acceptance of the gift is of equal importance to giving with a free heart. The gifts may be symbolic, linking donor and recipient in the promise of a richer and more gratifying intimacy.

When the Eight is in the upper left wing of the spread, the Querent will be the recipient of a gift which will have deep meaning for him if he makes the effort to understand its significance. If he spurns the gift or treats it lightly, his action may be followed by regret, for the gift can be the forerunner of many good things that can come his way.

When the Eight of Hearts appears in the lower left wing of the spread, the gift is much more likely to have intrinsic value and to come from a source which is not intimately connected with the Querent's life.

When the Eight is in the upper right-hand wing, the Querent will be the donor of the gift. If he gives openly and freely, without expectation of material reward, he will receive much gratification from the act. On the other hand, if he is prompted by greed, the gift may backfire and do him injury.

When the Eight is in the lower left wing, the indication is that the Querent will be able to help, or do a service for, a relative stranger. By so doing, he will eventually be amply repaid.

However, a warning should be issued to the Querent that the Eight of Hearts, when badly placed in the spread, can refer to a bribe, either offered or received. Such a gift should be rejected firmly lest it bring disgrace and ultimate tragedy to the recipient.

29. The Seven of Hearts

Traditionally the Seven of Hearts denotes a lover's quarrel. It is also a card of credulity and faith symbolized by the linked hands of children. The quarrel may be no more than a tiff which can clear the air for a better understanding between the participants. However, where the Seven of Hearts appears, it is wise to warn the Querent of a situation in which he should guard his temper lest words spoken in anger should form a permanent rift between himself and someone whom he loves.

The phrase "lover's quarrel" should not be taken too literally. The card may indicate a disagreement between any two people who are devoted to each other such as husband and wife, mother and daughter, or intimate friends. Where passions are unleashed the quarrel may become serious. The presence of the Nine or Ten of Spades or the Ten of Clubs close to the Seven of Hearts is a danger warning, signalling the Querent to guard his tongue.

Where the Seven of Hearts appears in the middle of the spread, the indication is that the Querent is too trustful, too content to let matters run their own course. Thoughtlessness or indolence may cause the loss of cherished friendships or happiness. He should take steps to reaffirm his love or affection for those whose warm regard is important to him. He should not take friendships, family intimacies and continued love for granted.

When the Seven of Hearts appears in either left wing of the spread, the indication is that another person has need of the Querent's strength and cherishing. If the card is in the lower left wing, the person dependent upon the Querent may be shy, inarticulate or so in awe of the Querent that he or she is incapable of making his needs known. Because of this, such a person may cloak his affection with sharp words or criticism. The Querent should be advised to deal gently with the situation so that no discord of a permanent nature arises.

If the Seven of Hearts appears in the right-hand side of the spread, the situation is reversed. The Querent may have a deep affection for or a dependency upon another individual, which he attempts to conceal or to which he gives inadequate thought. In this case the Querent should be warned against carping criticism, nagging or other undesirable means of attracting the attention of the love object. Instead, he should take constructive measures to strengthen the relationship. Honest appreciation and frankness of purpose will serve the Querent better than more devious means of securing the rapport which he desires.

30. The Six of Hearts

The symbol of the Six of Hearts is a flight of stairs which the Querent may ascend on his way to happiness. The stairway is only part of an elaborate maze which leads to success, the fulfilment of ambition, or the achievement of enduring love.

Usually the stairway can be climbed only through hard work, self-sacrifice or the setting aside of immediate plans. It may appear to the Querent that the effort is not worthwhile, that the promised rewards are not sufficiently great.

The Six of Hearts marks gain, an advance towards a desired goal, but not its immediate accomplishment. Therefore the Querent may feel disappointment at the partial fulfilment of his desires. He should be cautioned against impatience, irritability and a sense of frustration. Should he seek an easier route to the end he desires, he risks total failure.

If the Six of Hearts lies in the middle of the spread, the Querent will be called upon to make a decision in the near future. If this card lies in the upper left wing, his decision will be optional and the Reader should examine the right-hand wing to test the advisability of an alternate route. If the Six of Hearts lies in either of the lower wings, the stairway may lead to a specific opportunity which is to the Querent's advantage although it will have only a temporary effect on his life.

31. The Five of Hearts

The Five of Hearts is a card of disappointment, tears and vain regret. It may mark the end of a love affair or the abandonment of a cherished plan, but the sorrow seldom lies deep. Inwardly, the Querent has always known the illusory quality of the situation and that it could not endure. His vanity may be pricked, but he is unlikely to receive permanent scars from his unfortunate encounter. He may grieve briefly but, even as he does so, he cannot be unaware of a sense of relief at· his release from a self-imposed bondage.

The end of an unsatisfying romantic attachment, the breaking up of a one-sided friendship or the recognition that an ambition is impractical and impossible of achievement will clear the pathway to more sensible efforts and goals.

The Reader should not belittle a sense of loss, especially if the Querent reacts emotionally. Instead, he should aid the Querent in placing the unfortunate incident in correct perspective, so that it will act as a stepping stone towards more enduring interpersonal relationships and sounder judgments in planning for the future.

32. The Four of Hearts

The Four of Hearts offers an opportunity for happiness through work. This does not necessarily mean through the pursuit of one's vocation, although this may be the case. Essentially the Four of Hearts is a card of self-abnegation in which the interests of others are placed above one's own.

Its presence in the spread is indicative of opportunity, rather than the promise of increased pleasure. Within the Four of Hearts lies the element of choice. It presupposes an interest in humanity and a willingness to make sacrifices for others. The rewards are unlikely to be financial, but a route will open by which the Querent can enrich his life through service to others. If the Four of Hearts lies in the middle of the spread, the opportunity is already present. It is probable that initial steps have been taken in this direction.

Often where the Four of Hearts is present, the opportunity lies within the working pattern of the Querent. It may be that more of his time can be devoted to non-profit causes which will benefit others, or it may be that his leisure can be utilized in ways which will be helpful to others.

In some cases the Four of Hearts represents children or very young people. There is an intimation that work with youth groups, community enterprises or school organizations will give deep pleasure to the Querent.

As in most cards, there is a duality or reversal of meaning. Thus the Four of Hearts may represent happiness through association with elderly people.

While the motivation should not be financial gain, profit is not necessarily ruled out. Where Diamonds flank the Four this new interest may lead to better business opportunities, increased salary or unexpected gifts. Where there is a preponderance of Clubs in the spread, the road will be open for new and treasured social contacts. If Hearts or face cards are closely linked with the Four of Hearts, new friendships will be established, a sense of added security may develop and there is the possibility of romance.

33. The Three of Hearts

The Three of Hearts represents a disappointment in love, a minor setback in one's plans or an error in judgment. The appearance of the Three of Hearts is a warning that the pathway ahead is not straight, that there are pitfalls lying there to trip the unwary.

The Three of Hearts may also warn of self-delusion. The Querent may have a subconscious knowledge that he is handicapping himself or causing himself unhappiness by his reluctance to make changes. For a variety of reasons he may be loath to face the situation or he may hope that minor problems will solve themselves. The indication here is that he should shed impedimenta which weigh him down. If he is indolent, vacillating or indecisive, the difficulties will grow greater until they become an onerous burden.

Inherent in the Three of Hearts is a promise of increased happiness, success and well-being, but these are dependent upon the Querent's courage and determination. The lover's quarrel may set things aright. The temporary setback may clear the pathway to greater success. An error in judgment, once recognized, may prevent permanent unhappiness or defeat.

Where the Three of Hearts leads to the Nine of Hearts it has particular significance. A decision must soon be made or a positive action taken in order to secure permanent happiness. If the Three of Hearts leads to the Nine of Spades, the Querent should be advised to prepare himself to take rapid action to prevent catastrophe. But it should always be remembered that the Three of Hearts represents a choice. The danger it presents is not so much one of making an error as of drifting into a situation from which it will be increasingly difficult to extricate oneself.

34. The Two of Hearts

Traditionally, the Two of Hearts is a love letter or a bit of good news.

Actually this card has far greater significance. It points out the possibility of unexpected pleasure, satisfaction or joy which can be found in the ordinary routine of life. Often this promise is overlooked because it seems commonplace, or it is lost in a mass of details.

Where the Two of Hearts occurs, the Querent should be advised to examine his everyday life to see if he is deriving the maximum values from it. He may be missing opportunities, worthwhile friendships or social success because he is so intent on distant goals that he is oblivious of his immediate surroundings.

If the Two of Hearts lies next to a face card of the opposite sex from the Querent, the intimation is that there is someone at hand who would offer love and devotion if given the chance to do so. If a face card of the same sex lies next to the Two of Hearts, it may mean that the Querent is overlooking a friendship which could be beneficial to him. If Diamonds flank the Two of Hearts, it should be suggested that the Querent search his surroundings for financial opportunities and promotion in business. Where Clubs predominate in the spread, channels for happier social relations lie open if the Querent will seek them out.

If the Two lies between Hearts, the Querent may be indolent or too preoccupied with the pursuit of pleasure to establish more enduring values.

Whatever the case, the Two of Hearts marks opportunity close at hand which can enrich the Querent's life. He has no need to shed his lofty ambitions or his dreams of the future, but he should be advised that opportunities which lie at his fingertips may be rewarding beyond his dreams.

35. The Ace of Diamonds

The Ace of Diamonds is commonly thought to represent money. Actually, this is a debasement of its original meaning. The Ace of Diamonds is the card of magic or wizardry. Inasmuch as magic and science were synonymous in arcane lore, the Ace of Diamonds may represent mathematical knowledge, engineering skill or a bent towards sciences such as astronomy, biology, archaeology and especially architecture.

Arcane knowledge also informs us that the seat of magic lies in the home. The true magician was a "builder of houses." The Ace of Diamonds is a card that represents constructive power. Through the centuries the spiritual wisdom attributed to the magician was gradually reduced to the chicanery of the juggler, the individual who could keep many balls in the air at the same time, who depended upon trickery to bedazzle and bewilder those about him.

The true magician is a builder of character. He transmits knowledge from higher sources. His influence does not lie in trickery but in his capacity to understand and interpret the life forces which surround him.

The Ace of Diamonds is not a card of ease, contentment or luxury, as sometimes supposed. It represents an unceasingly restless spirit and is the emblem of intellectual curiosity, energy and a dissatisfaction with life as it is, coupled with a desire to attain lofty objectives which will benefit mankind.

Because the original Tarot cards have been truncated into the current 52-card pack, the Ace of Diamonds represents a large range of meaning. At its best the presence of this card can indicate a selfless nobility of spirit dedicated to the welfare of humanity. At the opposite range of possibilities lies the self-seeking individual, clever and ruthless, able to turn every situation to his own advantage. Therefore, the Reader must proceed with extreme caution when the Ace of Diamonds is prominent in the spread.

The promise of creative power is present and, to the best of his knowledge, the Reader should guide the Querent into channels through which the greatest benefits may be derived from his talents. The youthful Querent should be encouraged to explore fields of science about which he is uninformed for he may find in such areas an absorbing lifetime interest.

The female Querent's "magical powers" may lie within the home. By nature she is a skilful organizer and may have the unrecognized capacity to influence others, especially in encouraging and developing the character, personality and skills of the young. She is an excellent teacher, but should be warned against a tendency to stress success instead of genuine accomplishment.

Where the Ace of Diamonds appears prominently in the spread of the adult male Querent, the indication is that he will soon have an opportunity to use his organizational skills to advantage. The "house" which he builds may be a business structure, the reorganization of a department, the amalgamation of companies or advancement of scientific knowledge.

When the Ace of Diamonds appears in the upper left wing of the spread, the Querent should be alerted to keep his eyes open for an opportunity which offers, or appears to offer, high advantage to him. Without this forewarning the opportunity may escape his notice. However, if the Nine of Spades, Ten of Spades or Seven of Spades lies to the left of the Ace of Diamonds, he should be advised to proceed slowly lest some precipitate action on his part bring about a catastrophe.

When the Ace of Diamonds appears on the upper right wing of the spread, the indication is that the Querent has either already embarked on some venturous plan or will do so shortly. In such case, the other cards on the wing should be examined with care. If the Two of Spades lies to the left of the Ace of Diamonds, there is a warning of delay. If the Ten of Spades lies to the right of the Ace of Diamonds, the Querent should be advised to consider other patterns of procedure. On the other hand, if Hearts or Clubs lie in close juxtaposition to the Ace of Diamonds, the promise is that some plan will have a happy and fruitful issue.

Inherent in the Ace of Diamonds is an irrevocable force. The Querent who seizes the opportunities offered by the Ace may find his life patterns changed. Usually these opportunities include financial benefits. However, embracing them may mean the sacrifice of values which, in the long run, are more deeply cherished. The Reader may find indications in the spread that a total absorption in some project may lead to losses in other areas. Where this is so, this possibility should be drawn to the attention of the Querent.

◇ A

ROI DE DENIER

36. The King of Diamonds

The King of Diamonds represents a tremendously complex man, subtle, artistic, highly intelligent, with many hidden facets to his personality. He is prone to quick temper, though he may conceal this to forward his own ends. If he does not, he will possess a biting wit which creates many enemies for him. He has the capacity for rigid self-control, but may give way to rages and even violence.

This man is a creator. He is possessed of a driving, restless force that will give him no peace but which acts as a spur so that he is constantly seeking some fresh achievement. He is a skilled organizer, quick to see values especially in such fields as art, the theatre, literature, advertising or business enterprises which require vision and quick grasp of ambitious plans. His failings are lack of tact, disinterest in detail, impatience and a tendency to underestimate others.

He is mercurial in temperament. He can be suave, ingratiating and highly attractive to women. However, he is likely to be cursed with a streak of cruelty, to ride roughshod over those who stand in his way. When he is in the throes of some creative passion, he will be completely absorbed, seemingly indifferent or even callous in his relationship to his associates and even his family.

Despite this he has a strong sense of family unity, especially if it concerns his children. His loyalties can be deep and intense although often shrouded by the appearance of offhandedness or overly sharp criticism.

He is a master of subtlety, indirection and intrigue, but capable of generous gestures and lofty ideals. Despite his appearance of aggressiveness, he can be easily hurt and he craves acceptance and a circle of warm friends. His moods may shift with lightning speed. Elation may be followed by dark despair and overpowering depression. Beneath his external self-confidence is self-doubt and fear of inadequacy. He badly needs someone to bolster his ego and a confidante to whom he can impart his soaring ambitions. While he may lash out at such a person in a fit of anger or frustration, he will later be contrite and will seek to make redress with exaggerated praise, expensive gifts, cajolery or elaborate gestures.

He is a natural born actor, though he rarely is attracted to the stage because he dislikes to take direction. He prefers the world as his theatre and throws himself into rôle after rôle. He is likely to be a man of excesses and should be chary of overeating, drugs, alcohol and other stimulants.

Where the King of Diamonds appears in the middle of the spread of the male Querent, the indication is that he has many of the attributes of this card. He should be cautioned to direct his talents into constructive channels, to guard his temper, to

63

establish loyal friendships and to avoid excesses and a tendency to try to move ahead too rapidly. Such a man has a great need for a warm, intimate relationship with a woman but his selection must be made with consummate care. He may find the ideal helpmate in the Queen of Spades whose outer calm, intuitive powers and recognition of artistic leanings in others will give him ballast in his periods of discouragement and will add to his sense of accomplishment when he has been successful. However, he is likely to prefer the adoring Queen of Hearts of whom he may soon tire, or the more frivolous Queen of Clubs who is less likely to offer him the stability which he requires.

The female Querent who finds the King of Diamonds in the middle of the spread, is either in close contact with a many-talented and complex man, or will meet such a man in the near future. It may be that the presence of this card is a warning that she has not recognized the soaring aspirations, the dreams, the hidden skills and latent talents of a husband, son, suitor or companion. If this is so, she should try to establish a closer rapport with this man, for she will find her own life will be made richer, more exciting and more meaningful by achieving a unity of mind and spirit with the King of Diamonds.

When this card is in the upper left-hand wing, the female Querent may have a choice of linking herself to the King of Diamonds or of keeping clear of him. In this case, she should examine her own personality with care. Does she wish to lead a turbulent, explosive life in which she must subjugate her own personality to that of another? Has she the stability, the tolerance, the generosity of spirit and mind to grapple with the problems which such a union will bring? She may help raise such a man to the heights of success, but there will be many disappointments and heartbreaks along the way. If she fails, she may do both the man and herself a grave injustice. This is the road which only the stalwart should choose.

If the Querent is male and the King of Diamonds lies in the

upper wings of the spread, the indication is of a close alliance between the Querent and a man of mercurial temperament. This may be a friendship, a father-son relationship, or a business association but, in most cases, the intimacy will extend beyond this. The Querent will be likely to act either in the rôle of patron or protégé of the King of Diamonds. This may be a fruitful relationship and one filled with promise, but the Querent should be warned not to be bedazzled by his associate's brilliance. He must keep his own personality and integrity intact, lest he become a puppet of a more forceful individual.

The King of Diamonds, when found in the lower wings of the spread, may spell opportunity or disaster. The other cards in the spread should provide the clues as to what the King of Diamonds may have to offer and whether or not it should be accepted.

When the King of Diamonds appears in these lower wings, he will enter the Querent's life for a brief period of time and then depart. If the Querent is a woman, she will not be able to hold this man, no matter how hard she may try. If the Querent is a man, he should beware of any impulsive action which may destroy the foundations of his business or his social or family life.

37. The Queen of Diamonds

The Queen of Diamonds is a fiercely passionate woman. She has great drive and energy. Her restless mind is constantly filled with plans, schemes, devices for making money, adding to her social prestige or controlling the destinies of others.

She is a woman who gets things done. The Queen of Diamonds can be an invaluable friend. With her agile mind, her indomitable spirit, her fierce loyalties, she is capable of directing those about her into constructive channels, to spur and goad them to success. She is an expert organizer, often interested in charity, social reforms or politics. She is aggressive and strongly partisan. She comes to the assistance of those in whom she believes with unstinting self-sacrifice.

At her best the Queen of Diamonds is a creative force. It is through such individuals that progress is made. When the Queen is linked to beneficient and spiritual concepts, her influence may be tremendous and her service to humanity incalculable. On the other hand, if she is linked to forces of evil, she can do untold damage. She is shrewd and clever, but her judgments are frequently in error. Unless her materialism is leavened with idealism, she may waste her talents on petty details and schemes. While capable of grandiose visions, she may become involved in bickering, spite and gossip. She must avoid malice if the richness of her personality is to reach fruition. She is in danger of being side-tracked from high objectives by her resentment of criticism, personal dislikes or undue pride.

She will have to combat her quick temper, her passionate nature, her tendency to act too quickly and to have too many interests. She has an affinity for flame-red, and like the flame she can bring life into quick being, but she can also destroy. Unless she takes care, she may burn herself out, so that the declining years of her life will be empty. However, this need not be so. If she establishes enduring relationships and worthy objectives, she can accumulate interests which will give her lifelong pleasure.

The Queen of Diamonds holds her own destiny in her hands. She can make her life rich, fruitful and filled with pleasure. But she tends to lack patience and insight into the motives of others. Unless she is careful, she will make many enemies because, in her desire to achieve specific ends, she may walk roughshod over the feelings of those whose friendships might be invaluable to her.

The Queen of Diamonds is inimical to the Queen of Spades. Where both Queens appear in the spread, there is likely to be a clash of wills. Because the Queen of Spades is more subtle and intuitive, she is likely to come out the victor. When such a quarrel appears in the offing, the Queen of Diamonds would do well to guard her temper and humble her pride in order to achieve her ends.

There is an affinity between the Queen of Diamonds and the King of Clubs. She can bring out his best points, help him bring his dreams to fruition, give him practical guidance and assistance which will counterbalance his tendency towards impracticality.

When the Queen of Diamonds appears in the middle of the spread of a female Querent, it is likely to indicate her own personality. The cards which adjoin the Queen emphasize or ameliorate the characteristics of the Queen. If the spread contains a preponderance of Clubs, the indication is that the Querent tends to use her skills well and for the benefit of others. Where there is a preponderance of Diamonds, there is danger of a too great preoccupation with money or other personal ambitions which may in the end impoverish her life. A preponderance of Hearts indicates an underlying gaiety and good will. Spades may indicate wasteful quarrels and a failure to achieve a maximum happiness because of involvement in matters of relatively small importance.

The male Querent who finds the Queen of Diamonds in his spread will be in contact with a woman of strong personality. She may be an invaluable ally, but she must be treated with consideration. She will be easily hurt, far more sensitive than she appears and, if she is offended, she can turn into a ruthless enemy whose skills may be employed to destroy him. However, once a true alliance is established, she will be passionately devoted to him. She can be controlled by tact and kindness and will make an interesting, challenging and often an exciting companion. The man who chooses the Queen of Diamonds for a wife cannot expect a calm or peaceful life, but he will rarely be bored.

Where the Queen of Diamonds appears in the outer wings of the spread, she is likely to be a woman whom the Querent will meet and who may play a significant rôle in his life. In such a case, the Querent should be advised not to offend this woman. She can be of great assistance in helping him achieve coveted goals and ambitions. But, if her anger is aroused, she may ply her skills to the Querent's disadvantage. When the Queen of Diamonds is in a wing and flanked by either the Nine or Ten of Spades, the Querent is warned of entanglement with a woman who will bring him sorrow or disgrace. When the Queen of Diamonds is flanked by the Nine of Diamonds or the Nine of Hearts, the indication is that the cultivation of a woman to whom the Querent is not quickly attracted may bring about the success of cherished plans or unexpected happiness.

CHEVALIER DES DENIERS   VALET DE DENIER

38. The Jack of Diamonds

The Jack of Diamonds represents an individual who is at the crossroads of life. If the card appears in the middle of the spread this person may be the Querent or another individual who is, or will shortly be, dependent upon him for advice or guidance.

While the Jack of Diamonds is usually thought of as a young person, this is not necessarily so. However, he or she will be an individual torn with inner conflict, temporarily indecisive, whose outer appearance may be misleading.

This person may be of either sex. Outwardly he may appear brash, self-assertive or overconfident, but inwardly he is seeking new patterns of life. He will be caught between cynicism and idealism. He will tend to conceal his ambitions, his visions and his love of beauty for fear of ridicule or adverse criticism.

This is a person of considerable talent who needs warm friendships and spiritual guidance, but who is likely to react to criticism by flying into a temper or rejecting the individual whom he feels misunderstands him. He is given to outwardly thoughtless actions, some of which may seem foolhardy or even cruel. Actually he is testing himself and others, seeking to build up confidence by departing from routine or the conventions.

The Jack of Diamonds is linked in Gypsy lore with "The Hanging Man." This is never a card of death, but indicates an individual who is "upside down," who is suspended between the realities of life and visions and ambitions which he has not been able to clarify. He is inverted, in a condition contrary to that in which most people are found. What he says and does must frequently be interpreted backwards, for he is striving for a wisdom which he has not yet attained.

His position is a precarious one, for in rejecting the conventional paths he "may walk in all things contrary to the world." Thus he can expect to meet outspoken antagonism and even persecution which may crush his spirit and deprive the world of the good he may do.

Any attempt to force him into conventional patterns will be destructive. However, he can be directed towards more concrete goals and a balance which will help him to achieve his ambitions. His recognition that idealism still exists in others may establish a sympathetic relationship so that he no longer feels that he walks alone. Unbeknownst to himself he is seeking perfect attunement with the life forces, and his confusion lies in the imperfections which he sees about him.

39. The Ten of Diamonds

The Ten of Diamonds is represented by the hermit's cell. It presages confinement or material bondage. In Gypsy lore, the Ten of Diamonds was often presented as a card of wealth which did not bring happiness. However, it has a broader meaning than this. It warns of too great a preoccupation with making money or seeking material success at the expense of spiritual neglect. It may also advise change, not so much of place, but of attitudes. Where the Ten of Diamonds appears, the Querent may be bogged down by boredom, routine, indifference or a lassitude of the spirits. He may feel that circumstances hem him in and that adventures of the mind and spirit are dreams which can no longer be achieved.

Inherent in the Ten of Diamonds is the means of escape from the narrow confines of daily life. There is the promise of a richer and more rewarding future if the Querent will raise his eyes toward wider horizons. The Ten of Diamonds warns of confinement or futility in which the restraining walls may be illusionary. Habit, self-satisfaction, fear of change or listlessness may impoverish the questing spirit and deprive the Querent of many joyous experiences.

Again in Gypsy lore, the Ten of Diamonds offers a choice of a journey over land or over water. This is not to be accepted in too literal a sense, although the Ten of Diamonds often indicates that an opportunity to travel is close at hand. The primary indication, however, is a choice between the plodding land route which represents financial gain, economic security and acceptance of a limited life, or of travel by water which symbolizes purity of thought and inner vision.

When the Ten of Diamonds appears in the middle of the spread, there is an indication of world-weariness, cynicism and an acceptance of a pattern of life that brings creature-comforts but lacks deeper satisfactions. There is an indication that a richer life is at hand but that the Querent must throw off his acceptance of conditions as they exist and prepare to take active steps in order to grasp opportunities which will be open to him.

The cards surrounding the Ten of Diamonds should offer clues to the nature of the way in which monotony may be broken so that swift changes can take place. It should be stressed that the Querent need not turn his back on his present mode of life, but he should achieve new vision to guide him to increased enjoyment.

On the lower wings of the spread, the Ten of Diamonds is more circumscribed. When so placed, it is likely to mean a pleasurable interlude from everyday living. This may come about through unexpected money which will ease economic worries, through travel or from an experience which will create new areas of interest. The warning, however, is implicit that the opportunity must be seized, or else the humdrum world will close in to form a hermit's cell.

40. The Nine of Diamonds

The Nine of Diamonds is a card of conflicting meanings.

Traditionally, it has been the card of wish fulfillment.

In Gypsy lore, however, it represents deceit, treachery, misrepresentation and danger.

It has been associated with the moon whose pale light masks the truth and gives answers which, while literally true, are misleading.

Thus the Querent who approaches the arcane symbols of the

cards to present a wish that is selfish, trivial or motivated by greed or vengeance may find his wish granted in a literal sense, only to have it rebound upon him disadvantageously. Like the ancient oracles, the cards, when flaunted, tend to mislead those who mock them.

On the other hand, where the Querent approaches the ancient symbols which the cards depict with respect, and his wishes conform to acceptable patterns of arcane law, no misdirection will occur. The truth will lie in the spread, but no single card will give a "yes" or "no" answer. The Nine of Diamonds is a challenge to the Reader's intuitive knowledge, his extra-sensory powers and his skill as a diviner.

Even when the Querent has been discouraged from making a concrete wish, he usually approaches the cards in the hope that some perplexing problem will be solved, some high ambition will reach fruition or, at the least, that he will be given assurance of happiness, success or good fortune. The Nine of Diamonds gives cognizance to the wish and indicates that in some degree it will be fulfilled. However, it does not promise that this will come about in the pattern which the Querent foresees, nor does it guarantee that the wish will bring satisfaction or happiness to the Querent.

The cards can guide the Reader in two ways. First, he must note the position of the Nine of Diamonds in the spread. If it lies in the middle, the indication may be that the wish is either pressing, or of supreme importance to the Querent. If it lies in the upper right wing, the indication is that the wish will be fulfilled in the natural course of events. If it lies in the upper left-hand wing, the fulfilment of the wish is possible if the Querent will reject his current pattern of life. If it appears in the lower left-hand wing, the wish is likely to be incidental to more important factors in the Querent's life. If it is on the lower right-hand wing, outside forces beyond the Querent's control will be the decisive factors. If the Nine of Diamonds lies on the outer edges of the spread, the indication is that the wish will eventually be fulfilled but only after many delays or disappointments.

The absence of the Nine of Diamonds is not a denial of the wish. Instead it indicates that no clear-cut answer regarding the wish can be given to the Querent. When the Nine of Diamonds is absent but the Nine and Ace of Spades occur in the spread, usually there is a direct negation of the wish. However, if the Nine of Hearts appears in the company of the Nine of Spades or the Ace of Spades, the indication is that, although the wish will not be fulfilled, the Querent will, in the end, be glad that this is so.

Where both the Nine of Diamonds and the Nine of Hearts appear in the spread, there is a promise of happiness and good fortune which will extend far beyond the wish. This combination of cards indicates a heightened awareness of life's pleasures, the gift of inward vision which will add fresh depths of understanding and a joyous frame of mind that can sweep away misfortunes.

41. The Eight of Diamonds

The Eight of Diamonds is a card of balance, indicating a combination of skill in financial affairs and a spiritual insight which will prevent undue stress upon material success. This card represents a practical point of view in which all theories are weighed and tested objectively. It is a card of moderation, tolerance and balanced strength.

Where the Eight of Diamonds appears in the middle of the spread, it is likely to indicate the character and personality of the Querent. In the Tarot cards, such an individual is symbolized by a figure standing with one foot on land and the other in water. This is an indication of the person's capacity to cope with practical matters without loss of vision or idealism.

He may be strongly attracted to chemistry or other work which involves laboratory experiments. He can also be invaluable in government service or in executive posts in which careful decisions must be weighed. The female Querent should be capable in family budgeting, a thoughtful mother and considerate wife.

When the Eight of Diamonds appears in the upper wings of the spread, the indication is that a situation will arise in which careful judgments should be made. There is a warning to beware of impetuosity and not to take things at face value. If the Eight of Diamonds lies in juxtaposition to a face card, the indication is that it will be advisable to consult some authoritative person and to obtain additional information before some decision is rendered.

If the Eight of Diamonds occurs in a spread in which Diamonds predominate, the Querent should be warned against making judgments solely for monetary reasons lest he suffer from loss of more enduring values if he does. Where the Nine or Ten of Spades follows the Eight of Diamonds, there is a possibility that the Querent will be tempted into bad investments by the promise of quick wealth. He should be advised to double-check any financial venture in which he may become involved.

The presence of Clubs in proximity to the Eight of Diamonds indicates steady gain, tranquility and the absence of pressing economic problems.

42. The Seven of Diamonds

The Seven of Diamonds is often a card of distress. It represents an unresolved problem weighing upon the Querent. Usually it involves finances although it may relate to domestic or business situations in which monetary matters are of secondary importance. Often there is a delayed decision. Circumstances which obscure the real issues of the problem make solution difficult.

When the Seven of Diamonds lies in the middle of the spread it may represent a problem which casts a shadow over the Querent's life and is preventing his progress towards the goals he desires. When this is so, it may be that the problem is not as difficult of solution as it appears, that the hazard can be removed or, at least, progress need not be delayed by the uncertainty which the dilemma creates. The nature of the problems will be suggested by the remaining cards in the spread.

Where the Seven of Diamonds is prominent in the spread, the utmost tact is required on the part of the Reader. If he notices that the Querent is unduly agitated, he should do what he can to calm him down. He should avoid giving too concrete advice, but should discuss the problem in general terms. The cards should guide him in finding material helpful to the Querent in establishing attitudes which will enable him to act according to his best judgment.

Frequently the Querent is voluble in his desire to discuss his problem and presses the Reader for direct answers. When this occurs, the Reader should draw attention to the strong cards in the spread, those that indicate qualities such as generosity, courage in the face of adversity, the capacity to form friendships, etc. The Querent should then be advised to explore the ways in which these characteristics can be used to his benefit.

Where the Seven of Diamonds appears on the upper wings of the spread, the indication is that a distressing situation may arise, but that it can be avoided or minimized if the Querent recognizes it in time. If the Seven of Diamonds is found in the lower wings of the spread, the problem may involve the Querent only indirectly. For instance, misfortune may befall a friend or circumstances may cause disturbances in his employment, his social activities or his business interests.

Inherent in the Seven of Diamonds is the possibility of advantageous solution. This card does not mark catastrophe; but a problem and the need to chart a course of action. If strong cards lie beyond the Seven of Diamonds, there is a promise that benefits may arise out of a period of discomfort or anxiety which could not have occurred otherwise.

43. The Six of Diamonds

The Six of Diamonds is a card of well-being, physical comfort and economic security. When it lies in the middle of the spread, it may emphasize the importance of these things to the Querent. The Six of Diamonds may indicate the comfortable circumstances of the Querent or it may guide him towards securing desired ends.

Frequently the appearance of the Six of Diamonds in the spread offers the Querent a choice between moderate financial well-being accompanied by security and ease of mind, or a more adventurous road which may be studded with pitfalls and uncertainties. This is particularly true if the Six of Diamonds is placed at the juncture of a wing.

If either of the upper wings shows routes leading to marked success or to misfortune, the Querent should be apprised of this. The choice may lie open to him to pyramid his success but, at the same time, he may jeopardize his security in the attempt. If the Six of Diamonds lies at the extreme end of the upper right wing, the indication is that if he continues on the route he is following, he will achieve satisfying results. If the Six of Diamonds lies at the extreme of the upper left wing, the indication is that an opportunity for change will arise which, if he so desires, may reward him with a calm, secure and comfortable life.

When the Six of Diamonds appears in the lower wings of the spread, its meaning is somewhat altered. The indication here is that the Querent should be alert to take advantage of a situation which can be turned to his benefit. This may be a business deal which brings him a handsome profit, the sale of property or a chance episode which can bring him considerable pleasure. If a face card flanks the Six of Diamonds, it indicates that such an opportunity may arise through his association with an individual whom the face card depicts.

In the Six of Diamonds lies the suggestion that the benefits offered may come about through unpredictable sources, such as the seemingly chance meeting with an old friend, a social gathering, a call made through kindness. Because opportunity may wear a commonplace mask, the Querent should be warned that hasty rejection of new responsibilities, or that irritation with old friends and routine work, may cause him to overlook means of securing advantages which may be of the utmost importance to him.

44. The Five of Diamonds

The Five of Diamonds forecasts a clash of wills. This is not to be interpreted as a quarrel, a lover's spat or an enduring feud. Usually this clash of wills will occur without acrimony. Indeed it may be so deeply submerged in the subconscious of those affected that they are unaware of the undercurrents of tension which run between them.

This will be a conflict of spiritual forces in which two people, closely united, accept opposing standards of values and seek different patterns in their futures. Outwardly the two people may be in accord, but their ambitions, their dreams of the future and their moral judgments set them apart.

This may occur in a husband-wife relationship, a business partnership or in situations relating to parent and child. Money may be involved, but this is not the crux of the conflict and it should not be permitted to obscure more important issues.

Sometimes, especially when the Five of Diamonds appears in the middle of the spread, there is an indication that the warring factors lie within the Querent. He may have two sets of conflicting moral codes or be torn with indecision between two patterns of living. This division in his personality may serve as a block to prevent happiness or success, causing him to vacillate or to negate his own accomplishments.

Inherent in the Five of Diamonds is the power to adapt, to reach a state of concord, so that the two lives can flow in harmony, each with the other. This does not necessitate compromise. Often conflicting points of view are not as divergent as they may appear. Sometimes identical long-term objectives are sought in different ways, and mere failure to interpret the objectives of another correctly may be the root of conflict.

The Querent who recognizes some hidden strife that mars his happiness should be encouraged to clarify his own aspirations and objectives, to set aside petty grievances and to concentrate on the moral and spiritual values which are of greatest importance to him. Once these are clear in his own mind, he may be able to present them to the other party in such a way as to gain their acceptance. Misunderstandings may be, to a large extent, the result of a failure to communicate with those close to him.

While the Five of Diamonds holds the promise of renewed warmth and strength in a personal relationship, it also hints at loneliness and separation if the warning is ignored.

45. The Four of Diamonds

The Four of Diamonds betokens concrete, measurable success in terms of finances, business or professional status. This is not a card of sudden fortune, good luck or sweeping changes. Instead it marks an advance earned by merit or hard work. This forward step may seem to have little importance in itself, but it will lay a foundation on which a series of other advances may be laid. The Querent may be inclined to dismiss his accomplishment as trifling, but actually it can bring him deeper satisfactions than he would achieve through more rapid progress towards his goals.

46. *The Three of Diamonds*

The Three of Diamonds often represents a legal document such as a contract, a will, a lease, or papers related to sale or purchase of property. At times it may represent a dispute over finances, wherein no legal documents are involved. It can also denote legal contracts which are not directly related to finances, such as marriage, divorce, adoption or other legal procedures.

The Three of Diamonds serves notice of financial or legal entanglement but, in itself, does not forecast the outcome. The card which lies just beyond the Three of Diamonds will give a clue to the conclusion of the proceedings. The Five of Diamonds in this position warns against acrimony and bitterness. The Seven of Diamonds indicates a solution to the situation which will be immediately displeasing to the Querent, but one which may serve his ends better than he thinks. The Nine of Diamonds lying beside the Three indicates that, while the Querent succeeds in his objectives, he may pay too heavy a price in achieving his ends. The Nine of Hearts promises happy issue from the contract. Minor Hearts indicate that the contract will be made in a friendly fashion, without dispute. Minor Clubs give promise that the document will lead the Querent into a more active life. Often when such Clubs appear, the indication is that the contract will deal with business and offer increased opportunities to the Querent.

If small Diamonds flank the Three of Diamonds, the Querent should be warned of placing too much emphasis on details of finances. Because of his preoccupation with a lawsuit or dispute over money, he may lose opportunities of greater importance. In this case, the wings of the spread should be studied for alternate routes through which petty annoyances may be avoided.

47. The Two of Diamonds

The Two of Diamonds augurs an unexpected communication concerning money or business. Usually it is a promise of a pleasant, though minor, surprise. The communication may contain a gift, a transfer of property, a legacy or an opportunity for a slightly better position. When blocked in by Spades, the message may indicate a happy surprise in the midst of adversity.

When the Two of Diamonds appears in any of the wings, it usually marks an isolated instance unrelated to the major influences in the Querent's life. However, if it appears in the middle of the spread, this communication will have far-reaching results, although they may not be visible immediately. In such case, the contents of the communication may result in a change of living conditions, meeting new people or the use of money in a way that will create fresh interests. The cards branching off from the Two of Diamonds should act as guideposts to the Reader in advising the Querent.

The Two of Diamonds, when prominent in the spread, may mean that a relatively small expenditure of money can give permanent pleasure to the Querent, and he should be advised to examine the possibilities. Money spent in travel, education, hobbies, club membership, or in any other way that will broaden the horizons of the Querent, may enrich his life far beyond his expectations.

48. The Ace of Clubs

The Ace of Clubs is a card of talent. It tells of high hopes and ambitions and denotes strong passions, imagination, energy and the power to communicate with others. Inherent in the card, however, is the suggestion that promises are unfulfilled, talents unchannelled, and the maximum of creativity jeopardized by inner turmoil.

When the Ace of Clubs is centrally located in the spread, it intimates that the Querent has been given high gifts of artistic creation, intuitive power, forces that spring not only from the mind but also from mystic sources. His imagination will be vivid and he will have the power to express his images through authorship in the larger sense, which may include communication through the written word, art, music, the ministry and a variety of other channels.

However, the Ace of Clubs also warns of the possibility of chaos. Too many drives may nullify one another, preventing the success of any. Keenness of mind, sharp perceptions and vividness of imagery may fail to serve useful purposes unless they can be given concrete shape.

The Ace of Clubs indicates a quickness of mind which is often accompanied by a failure to understand the limitations of others; an artistic temperament which thrusts aside practicalities; imaginative heights which lure their author away from solid accomplishment. For these reasons, the Querent should be urged to organize his activities and to perfect his plans lest he become a dabbler in the arts instead of a creative artist.

In arcane lore, the Ace of Clubs is sometimes linked with the nomad or wanderer who moves restlessly with the seasons, delighting in each day without thought of the future. Conversely, other arcane sources designate the Ace of Clubs as the master builder with the power to control the movements of the moon and sun and to change the pattern of the stars in the sky. In each case, the sense of exaltation is present and there are indications that the Querent who finds this card in his spread will enjoy travel, quick changes and variety, and that he will be deeply moved by beauty. Whether he controls these shifting forces or lets himself be carried willy-nilly through life depends upon the character and personality of the Querent.

The Reader should be guided in his advice to the Querent by the cards surrounding the Ace of Clubs. Where Hearts predominate in the spread, there is a warning of hedonism and a suggestion that the Querent may not have developed his talents because of his pleasures in daily living. Where Clubs dominate the spread, an interest and enjoyment in people and social activities may prevent full development of artistic skills. Diamonds indicate that material rewards may be gained by the exercise of latent talents. Spades may warn that the Querent is too easily discouraged by minor setbacks. A well-balanced spread promises increased pleasure and spiralling rewards through creative activity.

49. The King of Clubs

The King of Clubs represents a man of wide and diversified interests, outwardly sociable, but inwardly secretive and reserved. This man will not be easy to know, for his external appearance may belie his inner strength and his natural reticence may cloak his sensitivity and idealism.

The King of Clubs will have learned to adapt himself to the world about him. He may appear cynical, autocratic, harsh, or even unfeeling but, in his heart, he is a crusader, crying out against injustice and eager to help his fellow men. He has been hurt many times and therefore he has built a wall about his inner being to insulate himself from criticism.

This man will have many talents, some of which he may have developed secretly, not disclosing his interest even to those closest to him. Such a man will find routine employment or conducting a business boring and confining, but he may deliberately choose such work in order that his freedom be unencumbered during his leisure hours. He may even be very successful in enterprises which are distasteful to him provided he has other interests to satisfy his intellectual curiosity and surplus energies.

The King of Clubs is often a lonely man. The sympathetic

understanding of a woman will be vital to his happiness, but he will have difficulty in making his wants known. He is easily discouraged in matters of romance and, in consequence, often plays the passive role. He is susceptible to flattery and, although he will not admit it, tends to place a woman on a pedestal.

There is a natural affinity between the Queen of Diamonds and the King of Clubs. In her shrewdness, the Queen of Diamonds will bring out this man's good points and exploit his talents. Her restless drive will incite him to greater activity and her determination to live life fully will act as a challenge to his ingenuity and creative skill.

On the other hand, the Queen of Spades is inimical to the King of Clubs. Her haughty manner and concealed passions will deter him from the use of his talents. Where such a mis-mating occurs, both partners will withdraw to their inner recesses until no genuine contact exists between them.

When the King of Clubs appears in the middle of the spread of a male Querent, the indication is that it represents his own character and personality. When this card appears in the wings, it is more likely to represent a close friend, relative or business associate of the Querent.

When the King of Clubs appears in the middle of the spread of a female Querent, the indication is that such a man is playing a dominant rôle in her life. On the wings, the King of Clubs is likely to represent a man who will be significant in her life, but to a lesser degree.

A spread which includes both the King of Clubs and the Queen of Spades is likely to augur a broken home, domestic unhappiness or a marital rift. This will be intensified if cards which designate quarrels or misfortunes lie between these two face cards.

REINE DE BÂTON

50. The Queen of Clubs

The Queen of Clubs possesses the social graces. She will command and beguile the hearts of men, but none will truly understand her. She will be warm, friendly, charming, an excellent companion but, beneath her light manner, is a calculating mind, an earthiness, a quality of shrewdness in matters pertaining to her own interests.

She may appear flirtatious, light-hearted and giddy, but much of this is a mask. She is sensitive, easily hurt and sometimes petulant. She can be moved to quick compassion, but her anger may flare up unexpectedly and seemingly without reason. She will take quick likes and dislikes. On occasion she may conduct herself outrageously but she will soon be contrite.

Her actions will appear unpredictable, governed by whim or the fancy of the moment, yet beneath her inconsistent conduct is a feminine logic which she rarely betrays. She will be fond of social activities, dancing, games, travel and parties. She will be vain of her appearance, interested in clothing and luxuries. But despite her gaiety and laughter, there will be an underlying sadness that may show itself in moodiness, tears or tantrums.

She will love beauty, but her artistic judgments may not always be sound. She will talk easily and well, but her cleverness may be paper thin. She establishes friendships with great ease, but often these do not endure. Admiration is important to her; she enjoys being the focus of attention and responds eagerly to flattery. But she cannot be deluded easily. She sizes men up quickly and, while she may enjoy a romantic interlude, her decisions are based on practicalities.

The man who falls in love with the Queen of Clubs may feel that he is following a will-o'-the-wisp. Her moods are so given to fluctuation that she may appear to be many women rolled into one. In a sense this is true. Her personality will contain diverse and contradictory elements, any one of which may dominate in a given situation.

Despite her social graces, the Queen of Clubs is likely to cut herself off from close human relationships and to suffer from an inner loneliness. She has a deep craving for sympathy and someone who will understand her capricious moods. She is capable of tremendous self-sacrifice and enduring devotion to a man who can give her this, but she will test him constantly and, in the end, may drive him from her.

In her relationship with other women, the Queen of Clubs tends to seek out her own kind. Such friendships tend to be brief and filled with petty quarrels. However, the Queen of Clubs and the Queen of Hearts have an affinity for each other. The Queen of Hearts will offer absolute devotion while the Queen of Clubs will bring excitement, gaiety and diversity into their lives. The Queen of Clubs and the Queen of Spades are instinctive enemies. The presence of both cards in the spread indicates conflict in which the Queen of Spades, with her greater subtlety and intuition is likely to emerge victorious.

When the Queen of Clubs lies in the middle of the spread of the female Querent, the card may be either a representation of her personality or the problems which she will meet. If another Queen or Jack also lies in the middle of the spread, the indication is that the personality of the Queen of Clubs will be moderated by the characteristics of the second card.

When the male Querent finds the Queen of Clubs in the middle of his spread, a woman with many of these character traits will play a dominant part in his life.

When the Queen of Clubs appears in the upper right wing of the spread of either male or female Querent, the indication is that such a woman will soon be involved in his or her affairs. If the Queen of Clubs is in the upper left-hand spread, the Querent may be forced into some decision in regard to such a woman. The remaining cards in the wing may guide him to wise judgment as to the role she should be permitted to play.

When the Queen of Clubs appears in the lower wings of the spread, there is a warning that a situation may arise in which appearances are deceptive. The Querent should be advised to avoid snap judgments and not to be influenced by personality until the facts in the case have been thoroughly examined.

When the Nine of Hearts lies beside the Queen of Clubs, the indication is that such a woman will bring great joy into the Querent's life.

♣ Q

51. The Jack of Clubs

The Jack of Clubs usually represents a young person who is hard-working, honest and sincere. This card rarely represents the Querent but someone who is devoted to him. To determine the sex of the Jack of Clubs, the Reader should follow the direction of the eyes portrayed in the card. If the eyes point toward the middle of the spread, the young person will be of the opposite sex to the Querent. If the eyes point away from the middle of the spread, the person will be of the Querent's own sex.

There is a suggestion that the Querent may underestimate the Jack of Clubs, considering him naive, dull or lacking in gaiety. In the eyes of the female Querent, the Jack may appear in the guise of a lacklustre suitor or unprepossessing female friend. For the male Querent, the Jack may be a girl whom he knows well but whom he has not considered in a romantic light; or a steady, reliable male companion whom he takes for granted.

Actually, the Jack of Clubs will prove a tower of strength in times of crisis. He will be loyal, generous and self-sacrificing. He may possess many undeveloped or unsuspected talents beneath a rather commonplace exterior. Because he is content to play "second fiddle" to the Querent, he may deliberately conceal certain skills and aptitudes to make the Querent appear in the best possible light.

The Jack of Clubs may act as a rein on the Querent, checking his impulsive actions and guiding him towards his highest possible achievement. As a whole, the Jack of Clubs counsels wisely and is rich in common sense but his caution and protectiveness may become irksome and be resented. This is especially true since the Jack of Clubs is frequently lacking in tact. His natural honesty prevents him from the use of guile or subterfuge.

The presence of the Jack of Clubs in the spread is an indication that there is someone close to the Querent whom he does not fully appreciate. This person will promote the Querent's interests and work without remittance or expectation of reward to help him in the attainment of his ambitions.

While the Jack of Clubs is described as young, the adjective should not be taken too literally. The word "innocent" may be substituted for "young." The Jack of Clubs is usually found in the same age group as the Querent but inasmuch as he plays a secondary role, he may appear more inexperienced or ingenuous than he really is.

The fact that the Jack of Clubs makes his appearance in the spread indicates that the Querent should avoid a one-sided relationship. Cultivation of a devoted friend will give him added stability, tolerance and a rewarding experience. The suggestion is also present that a crisis may occur in which this friendship will be a decisive factor.

52. The Ten of Clubs

The Ten of Clubs takes the form of a youth, inexperienced, with a mind still filled with wonder at the earth's miracles. In this youth will be an admixture of lofty ambitions, uncertainty, an eagerness to experience life and a withdrawal from harsh realities. Because his character and personality are not fully formed, he will appear a mass of contradictions.

This youth does not represent the Querent but a person through whom the Querent may experience the fluctuating joys and sorrows of the young. Where the Querent has reached maturity, the youth may be a protégé, son or daughter, or even a grandchild. In the youthful Querent, the Ten of Clubs may represent a friend whose life is linked with his.

Through this youth, the Querent may enter into a whole new set of experiences, acquire fresh interests and re-awaken dormant ambitions and ideals. His life will be enriched but not all will be clear sailing. Misunderstandings will arise and clashes of personality. The relationship may appear one-sided yet, if this is so, it represents a failure on the part of the Querent. The youth is capable of loyalty, idealism, insight and clear intelligence. His questing spirit may at times lead him into misadventure, rebellion and acts which hurt the Querent or meet with his disapproval.

The older Querent should be cautioned not to attempt to remake the youth into his own image but to respect the system of trial and error through which the youth seeks to secure dominion over himself. The older Querent may advise, guide, open new doors for intellectual growth or assessment of values but he should beware of emotional dependence on the younger person.

Because the Ten of Clubs combines the significance of two Tarot cards, it sometimes has an alternate meaning. It may indicate that interests which held the Querent at an earlier date will be, or should be, renewed. The Querent may find pleasure in seeking out friends from the past or he may find that ambitions long forgotten will return. These interests will usually relate to some form of creative activity in the area of the arts, such as writing, painting, music or acting.

The Ten of Clubs is symbolized by a figure with one arm reaching back to the past, the other stretching into the future. The indication is of a new life, built upon the foundation of the old, which will form a continuity between youth and the years which lie ahead.

In Gypsy lore, this card was often spoken of as the card of adoption. Occasionally this may be interpreted in a literal sense, but usually the suggestion is of adopting new ideas, fresh interests and more exciting patterns which will enrich one's life.

53. The Nine of Clubs

The Nine of Clubs represents satisfaction or success in work. It is also indicative of emotional adjustment, stability and progress. Where the Nine of Diamonds appears in the same spread, financial rewards are promised. If the Querent works in the field of arts, the indication is of an important sale or contract. If he is in business, this may be a promotion, or a better position. When the Nine of Hearts appears in the same spread, the Nine of Clubs may represent recognition, acclaim or fame. The promise is made of happiness through achievement. Where the Nine of Spades appears with the Nine of Clubs, success is promised after many setbacks, strife and the threat of defeat.

When the Nine of Clubs appears in the upper left-hand wing of the spread, such success will depend on the immediate actions of the Querent. That which he seeks is within his grasp, but he must take the correct steps lest it evade him.

In the lower wings of the spread, the promised success is more localized, indicating a specific situation which can be used to his benefit and through which he may win financial rewards, fame or recognition.

The cards in the same row as the Nine of Clubs should give clues as to the nature of the enterprise, the people who may be involved, the obstacles which may have to be overcome and situations which will assist the Querent in achieving the ends he seeks.

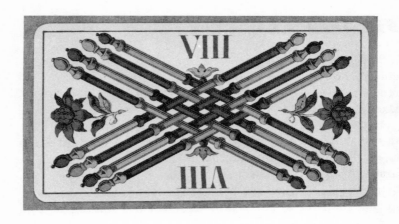

54. The Eight of Clubs

The Eight of Clubs is a card of balance, harmony and quiet delight. It indicates a questing spirit in search of beauty which may be found in such simple things as flowers, sunsets, books or friends. This is the card of the gentle dreamer but it represents only one aspect, perhaps a hidden one, of the Querent's personality. This is not a card of social detachment or financial incompetence. On the contrary, it suggests a clear recognition of values but, at the same time, it indicates a growing inclination to sacrifice material comfort for the pleasures of the mind and soul. The Querent who finds the Eight of Clubs in his spread is fortunate. He possesses inner qualities which will guard him from many of life's vicissitudes.

The Eight of Clubs holds a promise of a happiness that will increase with the years. Its presence in the middle of the spread may bring into focus the Querent's need to rely on these inner forces. This holds especially true if Diamonds dominate the spread, for this is a warning that financial or business concerns may usurp the Querent's time to a point where the full appreciation of life's beauty is blunted.

55. The Seven of Clubs

The Seven of Clubs warns of illusionary success, unstable effort and plans that may topple over backwards at the last moment because of carelessness, indifference or the too early assumption that all is well.

When the Seven of Clubs appears in the upper left wing of the spread, it indicates that some goal sought by the Querent is attainable but that he must exert vigilance, scrupulous care and unceasing energy in the enterprise. He must fight his inclination to resign himself to failure too quickly, be dilatory or lacking in self-confidence.

In the upper right wing of the spread, the Seven of Clubs indicates that the Querent is in danger of suffering a loss through default or neglect. It may be that he takes his success for granted or is too preoccupied with other matters to bend his energies to a task of real importance.

The Seven of Clubs bespeaks high aspirations, but when it appears in the middle of the spread it may indicate weakness on the part of the Querent in implementing his ambitions. There is an indication that he starts many enterprises but does not follow through. He tends, at times, to jump from one interest to another, spreading his energies too thin. Once a plan is well under way, he is inclined to turn his attention elsewhere. The card warns him that apparent success must be bolstered by hard work or his efforts may be destroyed.

In the lower wings, the Seven of Clubs is more likely to relate to a specific situation than to the general attitude of the Querent. In conjunction with a face card, it may warn of the carelessness or indifference of associates or employees. The Querent should be advised to check carefully on any enterprise in which he is vitally interested but which is being supervised by others.

When the Seven of Clubs lies between Hearts, the suggestion is that business may be neglected for pleasure. If it lies between

Diamonds, the Querent's security may be in the process of being undermined by financial chicanery or jealousy.

The Querent should be warned against disclosing plans indiscriminately to others and especially against announcing the success of his plans prematurely. Also he may convince himself too easily that he has achieved his objectives, and slacken his drive. His optimism may cause him unnecessary failure and exaggerate the blows of misfortune.

It should be stressed by the Reader that the Seven of Clubs is a warning of danger that can be averted rather than an omen of ill luck.

56. The Six of Clubs

The Six of Clubs speaks of opportunities for a burgeoning social life. Often it is referred to as the card of dancing and merriment but it does not represent thoughtless gaiety. The pleasures which it promises are partly of the mind and spirit, which can alter the Querent's outlook and change his life. In some of the Gypsy packs, the Six of Clubs indicates a journey and a change of abode. But the journey may be within the mind and the change of abode may represent a difference in the Querent's thoughts, attitudes and general outlook.

Usually the Six of Clubs is a card of good fortune in which spiralling social prestige brings with it other advantages such as financial benefits, increased security and the possibility of love.

In the Tarot cards, the Six of Clubs is sometimes represented by a merchant giving alms to beggars, an indication of his success as well as his goodness of heart, but the card also gives a warning against vanity, patronizing attitudes and jealousy.

If the Ten of Spades, the Two of Spades, or the Five of Diamonds lies beside the Six of Clubs, care should be taken to establish a proper balance between the quest for pleasure and the more serious aspects of life in order that they may be blended into a harmonious whole.

57. The Five of Clubs

The Five of Clubs warns that care must be taken to avoid a rift between old friends. There is danger of a quarrel that will cause the Querent grief unless he takes steps to prevent it. This is not a lover's tiff or a disagreement between husband and wife. The quarrel is much more likely to be between the Querent and a person of his own sex, unless a face card representing the opposite sex lies next to the Five of Clubs.

This card symbolizes rivalry, competition, strife and jealousy. It warns the Querent not to flaunt his own success or to resent the social success of others. Should the Five of Clubs appear in the middle of the spread, the Querent may find hidden hostilities among his associates which he does not suspect. Unless he guards his temper and shows unusual consideration, he may suffer a social setback and alienate individuals whose friendships he cherishes. The prominence of the position of the card in the spread is an indication of the serious after-effects of a quarrel which may seem insignificant in its early stages.

If the Five of Clubs appears on the upper wings of the spread, the quarrel is one which can be avoided, and the other cards in the wing should direct the Reader in guiding the Querent away from a situation which can only bring sorrow and regret.

If the Five of Clubs appears on the lower wings of the spread, the quarrel is much more likely to relate to a specific matter. In this case the ill will of another, not necessarily an intimate, may cause the Querent to be disappointed in some project of a social nature which is of importance to him. In the lower left wing, this lack of success may spring from a set of circumstances for which no one individual is responsible and, if this is the case, the Querent should be warned not to attempt to place blame. Actually a seeming loss of prestige may have beneficial results, which may be made known through the cards adjoining the Five of Clubs.

58. The Four of Clubs

The Four of Clubs is a card of strengthening friendships and increased social capacities. It suggests that the Querent is held in warm affection and high regard by those about him but that he is not fully aware of this cherishing. The intimation is that, in case of need, he may find assistance from unexpected sources.

This card represents gradual growth, a day by day tightening of bonds of affection which may escape the Querent's notice. There is a hint that the Querent may feel forlorn or abandoned, but, if so, his loneliness is self-imposed. Modesty, shyness or inarticulateness may prevent the full pleasure of friendships which are available to him. If this is the case, the Querent should be advised that open friendliness on his part, together with a kindly interest in those about him, may open up gates to more rewarding social activities.

There is a suggestion that the Querent underestimates himself and that he is capable of inspiring unexpected depths of friendship and of being deemed worthy of loyalties. A fuller recognition of the regard in which he is held by others may enrich the Querent's life, but it should be counterbalanced by a more searching attempt on his part to find greater values and admirable characteristics in his associates.

59. The Three of Clubs

The Three of Clubs indicates an unpleasant social episode. This may be a snub, a slight or a bit of malicious gossip. In itself, such an incident is unlikely to be important but the presence of the card in the spread, especially in a major position, is a warning to the Querent that his reaction to this unpleasantness may be out of proportion to the original harm done. He should use the utmost care not to let injured pride or outraged sensitivities lead him into vituperation, vindictiveness or unseemly actions. Should he do so, the ill will which results may do him serious injury.

The Querent would do well to assess the situation calmly and reasonably. The slight may be unintentional or the gossip exaggerated as it is relayed to him. The surrounding cards may even show that capable handling of the incident may eventuate in its being turned to the Querent's benefit. Particular care should be taken if Hearts lie at one side of the Three of Clubs and Spades at the other. Here a choice is indicated, showing that restraint and generosity will lead to a happy conclusion, while anger and unrestrained passions can inflame a minor unpleasantness until it threatens the Querent's happiness.

60. The Two of Clubs

The Two of Clubs represents a social invitation. This may be a bid to a club, an invitation to a social gathering or even a dinner engagement. On the surface this invitation may seem trifling, of little consequence. But the appearance of the Two of Clubs in the spread indicates that the acceptance of the invitation will play an unexpectedly important role in the Querent's life. This is particularly true if the card lies in the middle of the spread. When face cards appear close to the Two of Clubs, the indication is that this invitation will lead to new friendships. If a face card representing an individual of the opposite sex from the Querent lies directly above or below the Two of Clubs, there is a promise of romantic attachment springing from some social gathering.

If the Two of Clubs lies in a spread in which Diamonds predominate, the acceptance of this invitation promises financial rewards. Should the Ten of Spades block the path of the Two of Clubs, the Querent should be warned that the acceptance of the invitation may have unpleasant results and that refusal may be advisable. When Hearts predominate in the spread, the Two of Clubs suggests that this invitation will open a path to many things which the Querent has long desired. The presence of other Clubs close to the Two hints at gaiety, pleasure and social activity which result from the acceptance of the casual invitation.

61. Three and Four of a Kind

When pairs of cards appear in the spread, there is usually little significance except that the importance of each card may be magnified to some degree by the presence of the other. However, when three or four cards of the same numerical value appear in the spread, a specific meaning may be attached beyond the significance of the individual cards, as follows.

4 Aces=Great power and force, dynamic action, radical changes.

3 Aces=Opportunities, movement, fresh interests, success beyond expectation in some enterprise.

(*a*) Lacking the Ace of Spades, these interests promise great pleasure, new friends, joy without regret.

(*b*) Lacking the Ace of Hearts, these activities do not relate to love or domesticity.

(*c*) Lacking the Ace of Diamonds, these activities will relate in a minor degree to business or finance.

(*d*) Lacking the Ace of Clubs, these activities will affect the Querent's social life very little.

4 Kings=*For male Querent:* New associations, an enlarged circle of friends or business acquaintances, prizes, respect, fresh responsibilities.

For female Querent: New and involved relationships with men, possibilities of domestic entanglements, jealousies.

3 Kings=*For male Querent:* Fresh business contacts, male pleasures. With three rather than four Kings: less likelihood of unpleasant involvements or burdensome duties, greater promise of enjoyment and increased success.

For female Querent: An enlarged circle of male friends, possibilities of romantic attachment, a heightened awareness of her own femininity. With three rather than four Kings: less likelihood of quarrels, jealousies and unpleasant entanglements; greater promise of permanent pleasure in new friends.

4 Queens=*For male Querent:* A situation which may be embarrassing, comic or even ribald. A suggestion that he will be involved in intense jealousies and he should be advised against taking himself too seriously. He may be torn by conflicting loyalties but can be saved by a sense of humor in regard to his own attraction for women.

For female Querent: Gossip. A warning that her affairs are a focus of interest among other women. She should be advised to treat what may appear as undue interference from friends with lightness and good humor for, if she is hurt by idle talk, she may cause herself great unhappiness.

3 Queens=Meetings with important people. Whether male or female, Querent should be advised to cultivate new acquaintances among the women he or she shall meet in the near future, for these contacts will be richly rewarding. Also an implicit warning that the virtues of these women will not be quickly recognizable, but through sincere interest in them as persons Querent can reap the rich rewards of loyalties they are willing to give.

4 Jacks=Association with young people, the rapid approach of unexpected situations involving youth.

3 Jacks=Correspondence, news, messages of various kinds.

(*a*) Lacking the Jack of Spades, the news will be altogether pleasant and joyful.

(*b*) Lacking the Jack of Hearts, the news will not relate to love or family.

(*c*) Lacking the Jack of Diamonds, the news will not relate to finances.

(*d*) Lacking the Jack of Clubs, the news will not alter the Querent's social life.

4 Tens=The Tens represent doors. The indication is that old patterns of life will close and new patterns open. Querent is advised to adjust to different ways of life, to take advantage of fresh opportunities.

3 Tens=The meaning is the same as with four Tens but to a lesser degree.

(*a*) If the Ten of Spades is missing: no unhappiness in the loss of old friendships or familiar ways.

(*b*) If the Ten of Hearts is missing: no radical change in home or family.

(*c*) If the Ten of Diamonds is missing: no radical alteration of Querent's business or finances.

(*d*) If the Ten of Clubs is missing: no loss of friends or social activities.

4 Nines=The fulfilment of long-cherished dreams, hopes, ambitions, but a warning that this fulfilment may not bring the happiness expected. Querent should guard himself against unexpected disappointments.

3 Nines=Happiness coming from unexpected sources; wishes fulfilled. Perhaps a turn of fate which seems to threaten disaster will ironically end in pleasure and success.

4 Eights=Balance and adjustment in daily life, calm pleasure; a blending of material comfort and spiritual insight.

3 Eights=An increased capacity to deal with difficulties and still enjoy life. Forbearance. Strengthened character. Inward pleasure unaffected by chance or misfortune.

4 Sevens=Danger of conflict, quarrels, disappointments. A warning of the necessity for restraint, quiet courage and devotion to duty in the face of difficulty.

3 Sevens=Bickering, petty gossip, possibility of false accusations. Querent is warned not to be misdirected from high purposes, to ignore unfairness and jealousy, so that when truth is established, he may benefit by his own integrity.

4 Sixes=Slow, steady progress toward desired goals and suggestion that Querent is being tested; warn against impatience.

3 Sixes=Hidden opportunities. The indication is that judgment on Querent has been temporarily suspended, that if he acquits himself well in minor matters, his actions will terminate in more satisfying friendships, promotion in business or other benefits.

4 Fives=Orderliness, absorption in detail, rigid adherence to routine. An intimation that Querent may be deprived of many of life's pleasures unless he can break with established customs and seek fresh outlooks.

3 Fives=Revolt against authority, but unconsidered judgment may result in loss of prestige, waste of energy over trivialities. Querent should be advised to weigh any action to make certain his goals are worthy as well as workable.

4 Fours=Rest, peace, changelessness. An intimation that life will be uneventful with renewed satisfactions in daily living.

3 Fours=Hardships overcome. Rest after strife, sickness or misfortune. A philosophical acceptance of limitations which will result in increased pleasure and inner calm.

4 Threes=Dissatisfaction, resolutions, new beginnings. Querent should not give way to discouragement, but bolster his future plans with industry and scrupulous attention to detail, and take pleasure in establishing fresh interests.

3 Threes=Error in judgment, disappointment and discouragement. Querent should be warned against self-condemnation, encouraged to formulate fresh plans and resolutions, gain new knowledge.

4 Twos=Many small matters, some vexatious, some pleasur-

able. Delays, trifling gifts, brief visits. Pleasure in reading, nature, the arts, hobbies.

3 Twos = The same as 4 Twos except that:

(a) Lacking the Two of Spades, vexations will be minimized, small pleasures will fill the day.

(b) Lacking the Two of Hearts, pleasure will be found outside the home, especially in casual meetings with strangers, unexpected kindnesses from chance acquaintances.

(c) Lacking the Two of Diamonds, pleasures will be found in intangible things.

(d) Lacking the Two of Clubs, pleasure will rise from inner resources, increased awareness of beauty, renewed interests in neglected activities, spiritual insight.

62. Preponderance of Suits in the Spread

A marked preponderance of any suit in the spread has a significance of its own. This is particularly true when any suit is represented by five or more numerical cards. Inasmuch as the face cards usually indicate actual people, they should be omitted from the count unless all three of the suit are present.

A preponderance of SPADES heralds unexpected events. There is a suggestion of movement, upset plans, confusion and change. In general, Spades are associated with disappointment, regret and mysterious forces at work which are beyond the Querent's control. However, Spades should not be linked with misfortune. Throughout the ages they have been cards of mystery, charting courses into the unknown. Spades indicate activity and should serve as a challenge to the Querent for, if he is forewarned, he may be able to use the forces about him for his own good.

A preponderance of HEARTS promises pleasure, gaiety, laughter and joy. Hearts are also cards of permanence, stability, good health and freedom from care. However, many Hearts in the spread can warn of indolence, self-indulgence, and indifference to the welfare of others. Hearts usually offer the Querent a choice between the calm inner joys of contemplation and self-abnegation or the more hectic pleasures of material gain.

A preponderance of DIAMONDS marks a preoccupation with money, business, success and prestige. The combination of Diamonds with unfortunate Spades indicates an unhappy outcome to the Querent's financial plans such as the involvement in law suits, reverses in business or unexpected financial drainage resulting from illness, frustrated plans, duplicity or misplaced trust. On the other hand, a combination of Diamonds with Hearts indicates that plans will proceed smoothly and culminate happily. Where more than Five Diamonds appear in the spread, the Querent should be warned against materialism and advised to cultivate a diversity of interests.

A preponderance of CLUBS promises a more interesting and rewarding life. Clubs are frequently cards of energy, enterprise, sociability and usefulness. Clubs indicate the presence of opportunities for new friendships, an enlarged social circle and the beginning of activities which will give added significance to the Querent's life. There is a danger, however, that too many plans may prevent the fruition of any one. The Querent should be warned to circumscribe his social activities in order to devote more time to the cultivation of a few friends and the implementation of his most cherished ambitions.

63. High and Low Cards in the Spread

The presence of a large number of Aces and face cards in the spread indicates radical changes in the Querent's life. This is particularly true if the remaining cards include a number of Nines or Tens. Where these high cards dominate the spread, each serves to intensify the significance of the other. These major cards give promise of important events to come and indicate that the Querent's life will be intimately interwoven with the lives of others and that he will participate in activities concerning which he has no current knowledge.

Conversely, if the spread is composed largely of lesser cards, the indication is that the Querent's life will adhere closely to its present pattern. In this case, the interpretation of each card should be minimized. Thus the promise of a letter containing good news should be interpreted merely as a pleasant communication; quarrels may be reduced to misunderstandings, and unhappy events may be no more than passing irritations.

64. The Absence of the Death Card

Arcane lore denies the actuality of death, claiming that death merely marks the passage of the spirit from one sphere of life to another. Therefore, death and birth are synonymous and, because their symbols are identical, only the most acute of Readers can differentiate between the promise of a more complete spiritual life and the cessation of the bodily functions. For this reason it is unwise for the Querent to augur death under any circumstances.

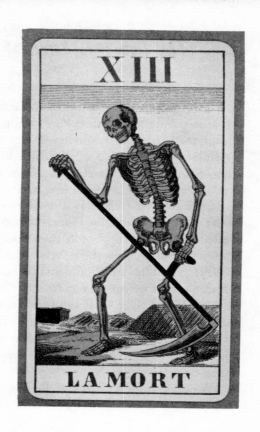

Similarly there is no card, or combination of cards, that foretells unallayed tragedy. The cards warn of attitudes, states of mind and personality defects which may prevent the Querent from achieving his highest objectives, but they only do so to guide him towards paths of his own choosing. The cards never condemn, nor do they offer dogmatic advice. Their primary purpose is to give heightened awareness to the Querent concerning the nature of his present and future problems in order to create an atmosphere of calm in which he may act with considered judgment and in accordance with his most worthy aspirations.

65. The Interpretation of Face Cards

Usually the face cards represent actual people. Inasmuch as no two people are identical and the pack is limited to a small number of face cards, obviously any specific card will not be completely descriptive of the individual whom it wishes to designate. Some of the characteristics of this individual will be lacking and others may be inaccurate.

If the Reader feels that a more minute description is desirable, he should ask the Querent to reshuffle the cards in the remaining pack. He should then select one or two cards from the pack and place them upon the face card. These cards should give him additional information about the individual characterized by the face card.

EXAMPLE No. 1: If the face card is the Queen of Hearts and the card drawn is the Three of Diamonds, the indication is that the Queen of Hearts is less naive than she appears, shrewder in business matters and possibly that she is prone to haggle over money.

EXAMPLE No. 2: If the Jack of Diamonds is covered by the King of Spades, the Jack is far less likely to represent a callow youth but one who has already started on the road to maturity and has absorbed, to some degree, the stability, integrity and dependability characteristic of the King of Spades.

EXAMPLE No. 3: If the Queen of Spades is covered by the Nine of Hearts, the indication is that there is a light-hearted, gay or even frivolous aspect to her personality. The assumption can also be made that her attitude towards the Querent is friendly and that, given the opportunity, she will be valuable to him in the attainment of the ends which he desires.

66. Sample Readings

A full reading of the cards usually takes about two hours. The Reader should prepare himself for the task by blotting out all personal concerns in order to dedicate himself to the welfare of the Querent.

The following readings have been greatly condensed. Each of the Querents came to me as a stranger. Two of them were recommended by psychiatric workers, who recognize that the Querent, confronted with the objectivity of the cards, will relax and often find solutions to his problems through this impersonal medium.

Sample Reading 1: A Teen-Age Boy

The Querent in this case was a boy, about 17, whose attitude towards the cards was noticeably sheepish. While we alternated in shuffling the cards, I explained to him some of their history and the significance of the ancient symbols which they represented. Only after his interest was aroused did I permit the first card to be laid down.

As the cards fell into place he became somewhat tense and nervous and it was obvious that he had a problem in which he desired guidance. The Nine of Hearts, I explained to him, offered the opportunity of great happiness, a useful, varied and exciting life. But this was an opportunity only, that he must prepare himself to seek wisdom and inner growth, and to approach his opportunity with the willingness to work and make sacrifices to bring it to reality. Many doors would be open to him to make life richly rewarding, but he must be able to walk proudly through these doors with the knowledge of his own integrity.

The two Jacks which flanked the Nine of Hearts offered a challenge in interpretation. It was possible that one of these

Jacks represented a person close to the Querent, a friend or sweetheart. But, as one Jack looked towards the Nine of Hearts as though to embrace the adventures of mind and spirit which it had to offer, and the other looked away as though in rejection, it seemed more likely that these cards represented warring factors inside the Querent, indecision, conflict and the need to take conclusive action to take full advantage of his future opportunities.

The Jack of Hearts which looked away from the Nine of Hearts, was a clear-cut warning that the Querent should take life more seriously, that he should not throw away future opportunity for passing pleasure, good times and lack of enterprise. The Jack of Diamonds, on the other hand, represented a person of latent skills and talents who was at the crossroads of life. The pathway suggested by the Jack of Diamonds offered many more immediate obstacles, difficulties which would have to be surmounted, disappointments and the necessity for self-abnegation. But this more difficult road promised far greater satisfaction than could be achieved by the drifting suggested by the Jack of Hearts.

In interpreting the spread, it was necessary at all times to take into consideration the Ten of Spades. This card, so placed, is a blocking card, representing an insurmountable wall or barrier. The interpretation here was that, if the Querent neglected opportunity and drifted thoughtlessly through the near future, he would ultimately find his life limited and his ambitions thwarted. A warning appeared that he must use initiative and decisive action to prevent this from happening.

An examination of the other cards in the wing was illuminating. The Eight of Spades promised a period of ease, comfort and pleasure, but also warned that these things would not endure and might leave the Querent's life barren and empty of intellectual stimuli. The temptation to take this easy pathway was made greater by the Four of Diamonds which suggested immediate good fortune in terms of money and temporary,

Sample Reading I

though minor, success which would be stifled, in the end, by the barrier indicated by the Ten of Spades.

As the drifting or easy route would seem to present disappointment and great difficulties in the end, it seemed advisable to explore alternate routes. The cards in the upper left wing offered a challenging alternate. The Ten of Diamonds is symbolized by the hermit's cell, but it is also a card that promises change, the possibility of travel, a different and more complex mode of life. In the youthful Querent, this card is likely to indicate the need for self-imposed discipline, the sacrifice of present comforts for adventures of the mind and spirit which are to come. It also should act as a goad for the Querent to grasp opportunities, to break loose from old habits and to dare to reach out toward higher objectives and a more purposeful way of life.

The Two of Clubs is usually a minor card representing an invitation which will result in new friends but, strategically placed in this spread between the Ten of Diamonds and the Queen of Hearts, it would appear to have a deeper significance. The interpretation given here was an opportunity for an enlarged circle of friends as well as new and stimulating opportunities for intellectual challenges. Also present was a suggestion that a path which appeared burdensome to the Querent would be filled with unexpected pleasures.

The Queen of Hearts lying at the end of the upper left wing has a host of possibilities in interpretation. Immediately suggested is the mother figure, wrapping the son in love and devotion, encouraging him to accept the more difficult route. The second intimation is more abstract; that of a benevolent authority, supervising and directing the Querent toward security and achievement. After careful consideration and getting *the feel* of the spread, both of these obvious interpretations were rejected in the belief that the Queen of Hearts, in this case, indicated that at the end of a difficult route lay the happiness, contentment and sense of accomplishment which the Queen of Hearts symbolizes. Also there is the intimation of a happy marriage, home and children. Where the carefree route ends in blockage, that which demands more immediate sacrifices holds the promise of a richly satisfying life.

Directly below the Jack of Diamonds lies the Ace of Clubs, a dynamic card representing high skill in the power to communicate with others, imagination, quickness of mind and creative activity. Inherent in this card is a warning that these skills must be developed and properly channelled if they are to reach fruition, and that neglect of these powers may lead to chaos in the Querent's life. Placed as it is in the spread, there is little room for doubt that the Querent possesses such gifts and that he should be advised to harness them for their proper fruition.

Beside the Ace lies the Seven of Clubs which is an additional warning that carelessness, hesitation and preoccupation with minor matters can prevent the success of long-term plans. The card demands of the Querent that he shall demonstrate energy, enterprise and constant vigilance in order that his highest ambitions shall reach fulfilment. It warns, too, of lack of self-confidence and the necessity of pitting one's self against obstacles in order that the full measure of one's capacities shall be reached.

The Five of Diamonds at the end of the wing intimates a clash of wills or a series of conflicting emotions and desires which must be brought into proper perspective before they can be dissolved. As no face cards were present in this wing, the quarrelling elements would appear to lie within the Querent. There was a clear-cut admonition to put aside relatively unimportant desires and settle the conflict on a well-thought-out basis. There is a warning that if pettiness, grievances, or immediate desires are permitted to interfere with moral and spiritual development, the Querent will suffer from long-term disappointments, loneliness and a sense of failure.

In juxtaposition to the entire spread, the minor cards appearing in the lower left-hand wing are of unusual interest.

The Three of Diamonds promises a contract, legal paper or agreement of some sort, while at the same time warning that too much preoccupation with immediate financial gains may, in the end, cause the forfeiture of greater values.

The Eight of Diamonds indicates that a decision must soon be rendered and also that the Querent will be able to cope financially with the problems which are of concern to him. It is a card that urges a balanced judgment between practicalities and idealism. Within this card also is the advice to seek further information and to consult more experienced persons in positions of authority.

The Four of Clubs which closes the wing is an assurance of warm regard on the part of others for the Querent. It suggests that he is not fully aware of the love which surrounds him or the willingness of many people to give him aid and assistance. The recommendation is that his fuller knowledge and understanding of family and friends can dispel a sense of loneliness and inadequacy on his part. There is also a promise of a growing group of friends and satisfactions which will develop when the Querent gains a fuller recognition of his own capacities and moves outwards to encompass greater responsibilities.

In brief, the picture presented by the spread is of a young man at the threshhold of life who is torn between his vaunting ambitions and high aspirations, and his fear of inadequacy and his desire to retreat into temporary security rather than risk failure.

Throughout the reading, the Querent became increasingly animated and, on several occasions, attempted to interrupt the reading to ask specific advice and to explain the nature of his problem. This was not permitted until the initial reading was completed.

When permitted, the Querent plunged eagerly into a discussion of the immediate problem which faced him—whether he should leave school to take a fairly well-paid job which had been offered him, or continue his education with the hope of entering the legal profession.

Although the cards appeared to give clear-cut answers to his questions, the temptation to give specific advice to the youth had to be set firmly aside. Instead he was advised to reach his own decisions by a careful weighing of his capacity to subject himself to the lengthy discipline required of professional train-. ing. He was urged to give thought to his long-term goals and to form judgments in keeping with his idealism and his humanitarian instincts. He was reminded that the cards suggested that he seek guidance from more experienced people.

In this case, as in many others, the objectivity of the symbols of the card was able to break through the restraints of the Querent, so that he was able to view his problems in a truer perspective and to cast aside his inhibitions regarding the discussion of his fears of inadequacy and failure.

His ultimate decision to tackle "the hard route" of college and legal training was not imposed upon him. His own desires were clarified by the use of the cards' ancient symbols and his determination was strengthened through contact with the wisdom of the cards handed down through countless generations.

Sample Reading II: An Elderly Widow

This spread was particularly challenging.

On the surface it indicated that the Querent, a woman of advanced years, was living a barren, sterile life, preoccupied with minor matters. However, in the right wing there was the promise of great happiness provided the Querent had the courage to break her humdrum routine. The problem was to lead the Querent into this alternate route without giving offense or exerting undue pressure.

The only face card, the King of Spades, lay in the lower left-hand wing, cut off by the Ten of Spades. This formation often signifies widowhood and that the Querent feels that her own life has ended with the death of another. The Six of Diamonds is the card of financial security, signifying a lack of economic problems.

The Ten of Diamonds in the middle of the spread symbolizes a cell or place of confinement. The intimation here was that the Querent found her life unrewarding and wished to cast off her fetters but did not know how to do so.

The cards which flank the Ten of Diamonds indicate that the Querent is bogged down in petty quarrels, trifling annoyances and minor disappointments. The right wing of the spread confirms this. The Three of Clubs is often a card of gossip, and the Three of Diamonds suggests bickering over money and pettiness. The Two of Hearts may be a card of good news which is so trifling as to be overlooked.

The lower right wing amplified the loneliness and dissatisfaction of the Querent. The Nine of Spades may represent a tragedy which can be averted and the Two of Spades warns of irritations and annoyances which may loom disproportionately large in the Querent's mind. The Six of Clubs advises the Querent to expand her social life if she would avoid boredom and stagnation.

Because these matters offered little that was of value to the Querent, they were passed over lightly to concentrate on the upper left wing of the spread. The Querent had considerable difficulty in grasping the meaning of the phrase "an alternate route." When it was explained to her that through fortitude and deliberate planning, she could alter her life, she insisted that she was too old and too set in her ways to make any changes, while at the same time, she complained bitterly of her loneliness.

The Six of Hearts was the first card to be examined. This card symbolizes a stairway to happiness. At its top, views of a wider horizon can be seen and there is the promise of fresh interests and a richer, more rewarding life. But to climb this

Sample Reading II

stairway requires effort, an act of will and a deliberate setting aside of old routines.

The Ten of Clubs was obviously the key card, which would provide the clue to the nature of the activity through which happiness might spring. This card is open to a variety of interpretations because, according to different schools of arcane thought, it has absorbed the meanings of several of the ancient Tarot cards which have been eliminated from the modern pack.

Frequently the Ten of Clubs symbolizes a youth of either sex, starry-eyed and visionary, before whom the whole world stretches. He is eager for experience and his personality is still unformed. In some cases, this card is illustrated by children holding hands.

It was suggested to the Querent that some such young person might be in her life, possibly a grandson, nephew or a child of a friend and that, through acting as a guide or mentor to this youthful person, her own interests would widen. Then latent ideals and ambitions would burgeon again.

The Querent rejected this interpretation, insisting that she was without friends or intimates. She also spurned the suggestion that, through charitable, religious or educational organizations, she might find pleasurable contacts with young people.

Finally it was mentioned that in Gypsy lore this card is considered a card of adoption. For the first time the Querent's apathy was pierced and she became animated. She explained that, during her husband's lifetime, she had desired to adopt a child but that he had opposed her wishes. Since his death, she had felt that she was too old and too much alone to make adoption feasible.

A prolonged discussion of the problems of adoption followed in which it was drawn to her attention that there are several organizations in operation through which children in distant lands can be sponsored, cared for and educated through monthly donations. The various sponsors can communicate with their "adopted children" by mail, send them gifts and follow their activities. The Querent immediately became animated, asking endless questions about these services. She secured the addresses of two such organizations and insisted that she would visit their headquarters the following day. Indeed, she became so excited that she left without waiting for an interpretation of the final card of the spread, the Nine of Hearts, which held the promise of happiness beyond all her expectations.

Sample Reading III: A Young Woman

The Querent in this case was an attractive woman in her mid-thirties, volatile, smartly dressed and filled with nervous energy. She shuffled the cards rapidly, almost violently, in spite of suggestions that she do so with thoughtful care. As each card was laid down she asked questions about it although it was explained to her that no divination could be made until the spread was complete.

The most notable feature of the spread was that the upper right wing was composed solely of Hearts. This was an immediate indication that the Querent's primary preoccupation lay in pleasure, romance and excitement, that she was more interested in temporary joy and passing delights than in calmer, more contemplative and more enduring pleasures. This surmise was strengthened by an examination of the individual cards composing the wing.

The Queen of Diamonds placed in the main line of the spread, facing the middle, was clearly the Querent herself. Moreover the traditional characteristics of the Queen of Diamonds fitted her. She was a woman of dynamic force, agile mind and fierce passions, who tended to dominate those about her and direct their lives. She was a good business woman, shrewd and clever, but, as the preponderance of Hearts in the spread indicated, she had a tendency to waste time in quarrels and to become too deeply involved in relatively unimportant details. The Querent readily agreed to this analysis of her personality and volunteered the information that she held a lucrative position as buyer for a large department store.

The Queen of Diamonds was looking directly at the Seven of Diamonds, a card of distress, indicating an unresolved problem concerning which the Querent was seeking advice. The other cards strengthened the impression that the problem did not relate to business or finances but was romantic in nature. The two face cards at the extremes of the upper wings indicated that she would soon be forced to make a choice between two men who were hostile to each other.

The inclusion of the Three of Spades on the main line of the spread, indicated that the Querent believed it necessary to make a swift, clear-cut decision which might cause bitterness and acrimony. It gave a warning for the need of tact and suggested that the Querent's actions were likely to be motivated by emotion rather than judgment. In conjunction with the Seven of Diamonds, it was clear that the Querent would remain in a state of inner turmoil until the matter was settled in her own mind.

The Querent's natural inclination was to select the road to the right which led to the Jack of Hearts, a card of romance which often indicates a temporary and unsatisfactory love affair. The Jack of Hearts, when it represents a person, is likely to personify a likeable, pleasant but somewhat shallow and irresponsible man who is so intent on a good time that he neglects the more serious aspects of life.

The Seven of Hearts is a card of lovers' quarrels. The Five of Hearts is likely to be a card of tears and vain regrets. When these two cards are included in a wing which is made up solely of Hearts, as they are in this case, they forecast periods of intense pleasure interposed with unhappiness, remorse, feelings of guilt, anger and recrimination. Such a spread also suggests

Sample Reading III

excitement, passion, moments of ecstasy and an uneven pathway filled with periods of elation and periods of depression, in which the future is never certain.

The alternate path, indicated by the upper left wing of the spread, is one which offers security, calm pleasure, contemplation and quiet joy. The King of Hearts at the end of the wing represents a solid, substantial man, mild-tempered and constant in his love.

The Eight of Spades suggests that this man can create a peaceful haven for the Querent in which she will know comfort and a state of well-being. The Eight of Diamonds represents freedom from financial worries and a life of moderation, in which pleasure will be allied with responsibility. This will be a smooth, well-worn path, free of emotional upsets, quarrels, worries, duplicity and uncertainty.

In the lower left wing of the spread are found two women, facing each other as though in strong opposition. The intimation is that they offer conflicting advice to the Querent. The Queen of Hearts is likely to be a simple, uncomplicated woman, deeply devoted to the Querent, but her judgments tend to be faulty, dictated by emotion or sentiment rather than wisdom. The judgment of the Queen of Spades will be highly intuitive and perceptive, but her advice will be offered bluntly and without tact. Moreover, as the Queen of Spades is inimical to the Querent, who is represented by the Queen of Diamonds, it is likely that disputes will arise between them, resulting in acrimonious quarrels and eventual estrangement. However, the Querent was warned not to flaunt the advice of the Queen of Spades through pique or spite, for this woman can be of incalculable assistance to her if a true rapport can be established between them.

The Six of Hearts, standing alone at the end of the wing, would appear to be unrelated to the main problem of the Querent. It represents a specific opportunity for success or promotion in business to which the Querent may be blinded through her emotional entanglements. Because of the proximity of the Six of Hearts to the Queen of Spades, it may be that this opportunity will arise for the Querent through the offices of the Queen of Spades.

In the lower right-hand wing of the spread, the Ace of Clubs lies directly beneath the card depicting the personality of the Querent and would appear to supply further information regarding her. The Ace of Clubs denotes high skills, creative powers and vivid imagination, but it also suggests unrestrained passions, judgments marred by emotional reactions, impulsiveness and inner turmoil. When this card is linked with the Queen of Diamonds, there is danger of sensuousness, quick temper and uncontrolled passions which can lead to folly, despair and, in extreme cases, to a life thrown into chaos.

The Six of Spades represents a period of anxious waiting, often accompanied by a feeling of hopelessness and inadequacy. The Querent may feel trapped by circumstances and should be warned against unconsidered action in a desperate attempt to break a seeming stalemate. The Eight of Clubs following the Six of Spades signifies that anxieties and disappointments which may appear bitter at the time, will later be recognized as tests of character, which will strengthen the inner resources of the Querent, and which will permit new and deeper pleasures that she will be able to evaluate with a higher degree of accuracy because she has escaped from a situation of danger and uncertainty. There is a promise here of a new self-recognition, an increased independence of spirit and a realization that happiness lies within the individual rather than in external circumstances.

This interpretation is further substantiated by the presence of three Eights in the spread. Eights, as a whole, are cards of balance. The presence of three Eights promises an ever-increasing capacity to deal with life's misfortunes with poise and equanimity. Especially when the Eight of Hearts is missing, there is an assurance of an ability to adjust and find happiness under any circumstances. There is also a promise of happiness in old age, a growing strength and a developing appreciation of beauty, especially in simple things.

In an overall analysis of the spread, a woman of strong personality is seen—one who is determined to live fully, seeking excitement, thrills and romance. She is a woman whose spirit cannot be broken but one who will dominate any situation in which she appears. She is given to quick judgment, tends to involve herself in complications and is hot-tempered, tempestuous, clever and wilful. She is faced with a choice: She may either set aside her inclinations and elect to lead an unexciting but secure and happy life; or she may pursue a course which will bring her many disappointments and much grief, but will also provide periods of excitement, intense pleasure, exaltation and rapture.

The accuracy of the spread can probably be estimated most clearly by the Querent's reactions.

At the end of the reading she asked, "Even if I pick all the wrong routes, I'll have some good times, won't I? It won't all be bad."

She was assured that, according to the cards, no pathway through life is without its compensations, that even grief, sorrow and despair tend to heighten periods of happiness and to make life more vivid and meaningful.

Her response was, "Well, that's the way I want it. I'm not ready for calm happiness yet. I'll take all the hard knocks life can give me as long as I can have some good times too!"

67. Summing Up

It should be remembered that the symbols of the cards have values similar in their basic concepts to the tenets of every major religion. Each of the four suits recommends certain virtues, and each number employed in the cards advises, in symbolic form, the adherence to a moral code in keeping with man's highest aspirations.

Inherent in the cards is a belief in a divine being, represented as the universal will to good, and the concept that man should strive to make himself worthy of being the vessel of this benign force.

Historically, the symbols from which those used on modern playing cards descend were used as decorations in the temples where the priest and priestesses convened. They were omnipresent reminders of the code of ethics demanded by those who lived within the inner circle.

SPADES were symbols of personal courage in the face of adversity, inner strength, self-abnegation and integrity. They demanded the growth of the spirit, uncompromising honesty and rigid self-control.

HEARTS were the symbols of universal love, stretching upwards to God, and outwards to embrace all mankind, cutting across all barriers of race, creed and nationality. They demanded gentleness, sympathy, kindness and the willingness to sacrifice for others. Through these symbols the priests sought to shrive themselves of pettiness, malice, envy, greed and all other unworthy attributes.

DIAMONDS were the symbols of achievement, ambition, scholarship and lofty ideals. They established worthy goals to which men could dedicate their lives. Diamonds represented constructive forces, admonishing men to create enduring edifices and to transfer their mental patterns and visionary concepts into concrete form.

CLUBS were the symbols of the humbler virtues. They taught modesty, the rejection of earthly power and glory for subservience to the will of the gods, truthfulness, balance, continence, endurance, and uncomplaining submission to the arrows of fate.

The numbers from 0 to 10 provided a key by which those who read the oracles could purify themselves before accepting the responsibility of interpreting the sacred images.

0—(The face cards, especially the Joker) instructed the priest that he was linked with all mankind, both in joy and sorrow.

1—(The Aces) instructed him to make himself the selfless vessel of the eternal forces which control and sustain the universe.

2—instructed him to attune his mind and thoughts to the wisdom of the ages.

3—instructed him to steep himself in ancient lore, that his words might bring harmony out of discord.

4—instructed him that there are endless riches to be found in the realm of the spirit.

5—instructed him that he must be just in every circumstance of life.

6—instructed him that the beauty of divine expression can be found in all things, however great or small.

7—instructed him that the spirit of man can emerge victorious over all obstacles.

8—instructed him that he must bring comfort to his fellow man and lead him toward a vision of exaltation and grandeur.

9—instructed him that each deed and word should be weighed in the balance of eternal truth.

10—instructed him that he is responsible to the kingdom of the spirit which is embodied in his flesh.

To a certain extent, the contemporary Reader of the cards assumes the rôles of the ancient priests and priestesses who read the oracles in the temples of Toth. Naturally he cannot take

126

on all the responsibilities of the guardians of arcane knowledge. The cards can be used rightfully for enjoyment, entertainment and instruction, but they should never be employed harmfully.

This book cannot end without a warning. Some individuals may be tempted to use the information garnered here for personal profit. To do so is to debase the ancient, mystical symbols of the cards. Moreover, from a practical point of view, it is dangerous, for many communities have ordinances against forecasting the future where money changes hands.

68. Reading One's Future in the Cards

Many people will wish to use the cards as a daily guide. To forecast one's own future is far more difficult than reading the cards for another person, but it can be done. In this case the individual becomes both the Reader and the Querent.

When the cards are employed frequently, a time span should be decided upon in advance. Obviously, people who use the cards from day to day must modify the significance of the symbols. In this case, the promise of good news may be no more than a cheering message from a friend, while the misfortune may be a trifling disappointment or irritation. However, the wisdom of the cards can be helpful in preparing the individual to face the morrow, for he can be prepared to ward off that which is harmful and to take full advantage of that which is of value to him.

The frequent user of the cards is advised to spend some time in the presence of the arcane symbols to prepare himself for the objectivity required for a clear reading. Some Readers may find such props as a clear crystal or pictures from the ancient Tarot cards helpful in achieving this objective state of mind.

Tarot cards depicting The Chariot, Force, Jupiter, The House of God, The Hanged Man, and Justice.